Published in 1988 by
The Hamlyn Publishing Group Limited
Michelin House, 81 Fulham Road,
London SW3 6RB

ISBN 0 600 55583 6

Printed in Italy

Typeset in Monophoto Bembo by
Vision Typesetting, Manchester

Another Hamlyn title you will enjoy
The Spine Chilling Book of Monsters
0 600 55584 4

*(Endpapers) the eerie atmosphere of 13th century
Whitby Abbey provided part of the setting for
Dracula, one of the greatest horror stories of all time.*

the SPINE CHILLING book of HORROR

Rupert Matthews
Consultant Francis X. King

HAMLYN

CONTENTS

Introduction

A slight tingle of terror running up and down the spine can be a thrilling feeling. Tales of ghosts, terror and nameless horrors have been popular for centuries. It is almost as if people enjoy being frightened, just a little. Often the tales of horror are simply imagined. Some writers have been able to pursue successful careers creating frightening stories.

But there is more to horror, and to this book, than imagined spectres and terrors. Many people firmly believe that ghosts, vampires and witches are real beings. Some of these people have come face to face with the ghosts of dead men, or have been attacked by figures appearing to be vampires.

Sometimes apparently ghostly events can be explained away as perfectly normal events which have been seen under unusual conditions. Others, however, are more difficult to dismiss. Who, other than Herne the Hunter, would stride through moonlit forests wearing antlers, surrounded by a pack of hounds? It is unlikely that close friends of a recently deceased man would mistake another man for his ghost.

Of course, none of the horrors in this book are accepted as real by science. There is no hard evidence that they exist at all. Only eye-witness reports and the tales of badly frightened people indicate that such horrors have really taken place. You may choose not to believe in such things as are contained in this book.

But when you are strolling through a dark forest and hear a slight rustling, can you be sure it is only a fox? Or is it one of the hounds of Herne following the scent of its terrible quarry?

HORRORS OF HISTORY

The Curse of the Pharaohs

The ancient Egyptians protected their tombs with dreadful curses. Inscriptions and spells promised death and misfortune to anyone who disturbed the dead. Many people consider these curses to be nothing more than pagan superstition. However, several sinister events have caused some experts to take the curses seriously.

The curses were created by the ancient Egyptians because of their religious beliefs. According to the priests and priestesses, the soul of a

dead person continued to live after death. In order to ensure the peace of the dead, the body had to be preserved. The grave containing the remains needed to be filled with objects, such as beds and chairs, which the dead person would find useful in the afterlife.

The pharaohs and rich nobles had their bodies preserved by a process involving chemicals and fluids, known as mummification. Buried with the mummy were rich goods, such as gold jewellery and precious stones. It was to protect these valuables that the curses were created. The Egyptians also tried to hide the entrances to their graves or placed booby traps within the tomb.

The stories concerning the curse of the pharaohs began to circulate during the middle of the 19th century. Until that time hieroglyphics, the writing of ancient Egypt, could not be translated. As soon as scientists began reading the inscriptions on tombs and mummy cases, they realized that many of the texts were curses. Few scientists were worried by these threats from the dead. But events caused several to change their minds.

One of the best recorded stories of a curse taking effect began in 1936. In that year Sir Alexander Seton and his wife visited a burial ground in Egypt. Lady Seton secretly removed a bone from the body within one of the tombs. The couple took the bone home to Scotland and placed it in a glass case in their dining room.

A few days later a lump of masonry fell from the house and nearly killed Sir Alexander. Soon afterwards, footsteps were heard in the dining room in the middle of the night. Sir Alexander went downstairs to investigate, but the room was empty.

The ghostly manifestations became rapidly more frightening. Sir Alexander's nephew saw a spectral figure on the staircase. Several servants fled the premises after seeing a figure wrapped in white robes wandering from room to room. Events came to a climax late one night. Tremendous crashes were heard coming from the room where the bone was kept. Sir Alexander grabbed his revolver and burst into the room. It was empty, but not undisturbed. Many pieces of furniture had been smashed or overturned, but the case containing the bone was untouched.

For many nights after that, the Seton residence became the scene of terrifying phenomena. Ornaments were broken and fires started with no visible cause. Eventually, Sir Alexander took the bone to a priest. The bone was blessed and then burnt. Once this ceremony had taken place, peace returned to the Setons.

Far more deadly than the curse which dogged the Setons was that which was laid on a mummy case belonging to a priestess of the god Amun-Ra. The priestess had been buried in Thebes about 1600 BC and a curse laid on her grave.

The mummy case was excavated in 1910 and sold to Douglas Murray, who was visiting Egypt at the time. The day of the sale, the man who sold the mummy case died. Three days later, Murray lost his arm in an accident. When travelling home with the mummy case, Murray heard that the Egyptian servants who had loaded the case onto the ship had died. During the voyage, two fellow passengers also died.

Once home in Britain, Murray decided to get rid of the purchase which he blamed for his misfortunes. However, he asked a photographer to take pictures of the mummy case before he sold it. When the pictures were developed, one of them showed a woman who was staring at the photographer with an expression of hatred. Within a week the photographer fell dead for no known reason.

The mummy case was transferred to the British Museum for safe keeping. Two porters carried the new exhibit into one of the display rooms. Within 24 hours, one porter had broken

his leg and the other had been killed in a road accident.

Once in the museum, the mummy case continued to cause trouble. Museum workers thought they heard strange noises. And one night a watchman came face to face with the ghostly figure of an Egyptian priestess. The watchman fainted instantly from fright.

Finally, in 1921, two exorcists were called in. They inspected the mummy case and were overwhelmed by a sense of evil. Using all their skill and willpower, the two men exorcized the spirit. The British Museum has been quiet ever since.

Similar stories of death and destruction have become attached to other mummies and objects

The Titanic and the Curse

It has been suggested that the *Titanic* fell victim to the curse of the pharaohs. When this passenger liner sank on 14 April 1912, 1,498 people drowned. It was one of the greatest shipping disasters of all time.

An Egyptian mummy had formed part of the cargo and had been stored beside the ship's command bridge. Several witnesses stated that the captain of the *Titanic* behaved oddly on the ship's fatal voyage. Had he succumbed to the power of the curse?

taken from Egyptian tombs. Many people dismiss the events as mere coincidence, but others are not so sure. It seems unlikely that so many deaths and illnesses should occur by chance when an Egyptian artifact is handled. For instance, 20 men were present at the opening of the tomb of Pharaoh Tutankhamen. Within a few months 13 of them were dead.

Some scientists have suggested that the Egyptians poisoned the tombs and the rich goods contained within them. If this were the case it might account for the large numbers of archaeological workers who have become sick and died from mysterious illnesses. It would not, however, explain the ghostly apparition which walked the corridors of the British Museum.

The Vanishing Tablet

When Lord Caernarvon and Howard Carter opened the tomb of Pharaoh Tutankhamen, they found a small tablet on which was engraved "Death will slay with his wings whoever disturbs the peace of the pharaoh." Not wishing to alarm the workers, Carter hid the tablet. Within a few weeks Caernarvon died. At the time of his death, all the lights in Cairo mysteriously failed. The tablet has never been found again.

The terrifying encounter between a night watchman and a supernatural guardian of the dead which took place in the British Museum earlier this century.

Phantom Armies

Ghosts are often associated with places where violent or tragic incidents have taken place. Few events can be more terrible than battles where thousands of men attempt to kill each other. It is hardly surprising that many battlefields have become the scenes of famous hauntings.

One of the most tragic battlefields is that of Sedgemoor in Somerset, England. On 6 July 1685 the rebel army of the Duke of Monmouth faced the troops of King James II here. The rebels were armed with muskets, pikes and swords, but the royal army had cannons.

During the battle a large part of Monmouth's army found themselves on the banks of a river, while their enemies were on the other side. The royal army opened fire with their cannons and cut down the rebels before they had a chance to fight back. While Monmouth's men were being gunned down, several ran to the river bank and shouted "Come across and fight." But the royal troops stayed where they were and shot the rebels.

To this day, the ghosts of the rebels are sometimes seen and heard. Several people walking along the banks of the river have heard voices calling "Come across and fight." This was the desperate plea of Monmouth's men.

Tragedy lies behind another haunted battlefield. On 16 April 1746 the Highland supporters of Bonnie Prince Charlie were defeated on Culloden Moor by royal troops led by the Duke of Cumberland. The battle was extraordinarily brutal. Wounded and captured Highlanders were butchered in cold blood on the orders of Cumberland.

The dead Scotsmen were buried beneath large mounds, which can still be seen. Many people have reported seeing the shadowy form of a Highland warrior standing sadly beside one mound. But the most noticeable feature of Culloden Moor is a terrible feeling of sadness. Many visitors to the battlefield are overcome by a depression which lifts when they leave the scene of the slaughter.

Far older phantoms have been seen in the Thuringian Forest in Germany. In the summer of AD 9, 20,000 Roman troops were lured into a trap by German barbarians and massacred. The area of forest where the fighting took place is haunted by spectral Roman legionaries.

More extraordinary are the ghosts which haunt the battlefield of Edgehill. The phantoms are particularly strange because when the ghosts were first seen, some of the men were still living. The battle was fought on 24 October 1642 between the troops of King Charles I and the

Parliamentarians in the English Civil War.

On the Christmas Eve following the battle, local shepherds saw ghostly soldiers fighting each other in the sky over the battlefield. When news of the event reached King Charles he sent some officers to investigate the reports. Not only did these investigators interview the shepherds, they also saw the ghostly battle.

The flags of different regiments could be clearly made out. The officers were able to follow the course of the original battle as it was refought above their heads. They were amazed to recognize the ghosts of men they knew well and who were still alive.

A similar event occurred in Belgium in 1815, a few days after the Battle of Waterloo. Numerous witnesses saw infantry, cavalry and artillery fighting in the sky. The event seemed to be an action replay of the recent battle.

The fact that these ghostly phenomenon include spectres of men still living seems to indicate that at least some ghosts are not spirits of the dead. Perhaps dramatic events become somehow recorded in their surroundings. These recordings are then replayed from time to time, appearing as ghosts.

The spectral battle at Edgehill.

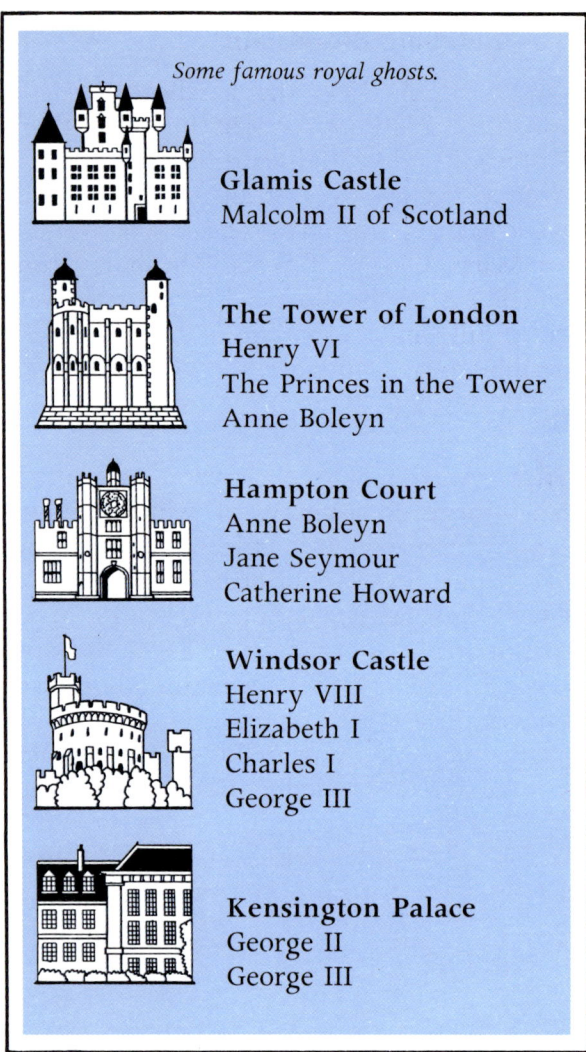

Some famous royal ghosts.

Glamis Castle
Malcolm II of Scotland

The Tower of London
Henry VI
The Princes in the Tower
Anne Boleyn

Hampton Court
Anne Boleyn
Jane Seymour
Catherine Howard

Windsor Castle
Henry VIII
Elizabeth I
Charles I
George III

Kensington Palace
George II
George III

Palaces of Terror

Palaces are the homes of kings, queens and presidents. The ghosts which haunt them are as famous as their living inhabitants. Some of these phantoms are so terrifying, they have sent people screaming from the buildings. The hauntings of palaces include some of the most horrific ever recorded.

A ghost which has a profound impact on those unfortunate enough to catch a glimpse of it, is that of Abraham Lincoln. Elected in 1860, Lincoln was probably the greatest president the United States has ever had. It seems that his ghost returns to the White House to keep an eye on his successors. The fact that Lincoln was murdered before he could complete his work

might account for his ghostly interest in current affairs.

When Queen Wilhemina of the Netherlands stayed at the White House she heard a knock at her door. She opened it to find the phantom Lincoln waiting to be let in. Queen Wilhemina promptly fainted. A few years earlier a valet of Theodore Roosevelt was so shocked by the ghost that he ran screaming from the White House, seriously alarming the guards outside. Other staff at the White House are more accustomed to Lincoln's spirit. They see him most frequently during crises which affect the president of the moment.

Far more bloody and violent are the restless spirits which haunt the Tower of London. For centuries, the Tower was both a royal palace and a prison for distinguished lawbreakers. The most truly horrific haunting of the Tower is the gory re-enactment of the dreadful execution of the Countess of Salisbury in 1541. The countess had committed no crime, but was sent to her death as an act of revenge by Henry VIII.

When ordered to place her head on the block the countess refused and fled. The axeman and prison guards gave chase. The countess ran screaming around Tower Green with the others in hot pursuit. Only when the executioner had struck several bloody blows with his axe, did the brave lady collapse and die. The vivid ghostly enactment of this scene has frightened more than one visitor to the old building.

Other unhappy victims of the axe also return to haunt the Tower. One of the most persistent ghosts is that of Lady Jane Grey who was executed in 1554. The ghost of this 16-year-old girl is usually seen walking the battlements at night on 12 February, the anniversary of her death.

On 12 February 1954 two sentries saw the ghost of Lady Jane Grey running along the wall near Salt Tower. Three years later the ghost startled a soldier of the Welsh Guards. The young man called a companion and together they watched the apparition for some time. More spectacular was the ghost which approached a sentry on a winter's night in 1864. A white lady emerged from the Queen's House and moved towards the soldier. Following orders, the soldier shouted a challenge at the stranger. The figure took no notice but continued to advance. The soldier pushed forwards with his bayonet, but the weapon passed clean through the figure. Suddenly realizing he was faced by a ghost, the man fainted.

Minutes later the captain of the guard arrived. Finding the man unconscious, the captain reported him for being asleep on duty. At the subsequent court martial the man told his story of the ghost. Two other soldiers offered themselves as witnesses and swore that they had seen the whole event. They stated that the figure which emerged from the Queen's House had been a ghost. The court believed the tale and the guard was acquitted.

Pacing the path outside the church of St Peter ad Vincula, within the Tower, can sometimes be seen the ghost of Anne Boleyn. This unfortunate woman was the second wife of King Henry

The Indelible Bloodstain

On 9 March 1566 the handsome Italian courtier David Rizzio was hacked to death in Holyrood Palace, Edinburgh. The murder was carried out by a group of nobles who were jealous of the favours heaped on Rizzio by Mary, Queen of Scots. The bloodstain which marks the floor where Rizzio was killed still remains. No amount of cleaning or scrubbing can remove it.

VIII. She was beheaded on Tower Green in 1536 on a charge of adultery, of which she was probably innocent. It is little wonder that her spirit haunts her place of burial.

The ghost of Anne Boleyn appears in far more dramatic and terrifying guise at Blickling Hall in Norfolk. Every 19 May, the anniversary of her death, Anne Boleyn sweeps into view. A spectral coach and four gallops along country lanes and into the grounds of Blickling. The four

The Tower of London, which has long been a royal palace and prison, is the scene of many hauntings.

The drive at Blickling Hall, where Anne Boleyn spent much of her childhood.

horses pulling the coach are headless, as is the coachman who urges them on. Anne herself sits in the coach with her head balanced on her lap.

The ghost of Anne Boleyn is thought to visit Blickling Hall because she was so happy here during her childhood. It is also thought that it was here that Henry came to court Anne during the early days of their romance.

Another ex-owner of Blickling returns on the anniversary of his death. This is Sir Henry Hobart who died in 1698. Sir Henry had been badly injured in a duel and was brought back to Blickling to be cared for. Each 21 August, the ghost of Sir Henry is said to appear in the bedroom where he died.

Far noisier than the headless Anne Boleyn, is the spirit of Catherine Howard which haunts Hampton Court, in Middlesex. Catherine was the fifth wife of Henry VIII and the second to die on the scaffold. It was in Hampton Court that

The horrific apparition of Anne Boleyn as she appears in a coach at Blickling Hall.

The King in the Forest

Royal ghosts are not confined to palaces and castles. One of the oldest regal phantoms haunts an area of forest in southern England. William Rufus was killed by an arrow when hunting in the New Forest on 2 August 1100. His body was taken to Winchester for burial. Many times over the years, his ghost has been seen travelling the route taken by his corpse.

the 20-year-old queen was arrested. King Henry was also in the palace and Catherine broke free from her guards and ran to Henry. However, the guards caught her before she could speak to him and dragged her screaming down a gallery.

Almost as soon as Catherine had died, her screams re-echoed along the gallery down which she had been pulled to her death. For many years the screams continued to ring out. Those who heard the piercing cries described them as both terrifying and heart breaking. The passion and terror felt by young Queen Catherine lingered in Hampton Court for many years. However, no ear splitting screams have sounded along the Haunted Gallery since the room was renovated in 1918.

But perhaps the most frightening apparition at Hampton Court Palace was that seen by a policeman on duty in the gardens in 1917. As the palace clock reached midnight, Constable 265T saw a group of 11 people approaching his post. He opened the gate by which he stood and waited for the party to pass through. The approaching group came to within ten metres (30 yards) of the constable and then vanished. Hardly believing his eyes, 265T rushed to the spot. There was no sign of a living soul. The constable took to his heels and fled.

Ghosts are not confined to palaces no longer inhabited by royalty. In one of the offices in Buckingham Palace the shady figure of a man is often seen. This is the ghost of Major John Gwynne who committed suicide here 80 years ago.

A ghost is also seen at Kensington Palace, where many members of the British royal family reside. King George II died here in 1760 while awaiting important news from Germany. As life slowly ebbed away, the king stared out of his bedroom window, watching for messengers who did not arrive until after his death. On occasional moonlit nights, the pale face of the dead king can be seen peering from the window and continually muttering "Why don't they come? Why don't they come?".

The palace with perhaps the most sinister reputation of all is Windsor Castle. Strange things happen in this ancient palace, which dates back more than 900 years. As recently as 1987 a guardsman on duty at Windsor Castle saw "something" about which he refused to elaborate.

But other witnesses are prepared to talk about the ghosts which lurk in the shadows of the ancient towers of Windsor Castle. Perhaps the oldest of these is the spectre of William de Wyckehan who designed much of the fortress in the 13th century. It is to be hoped that the ghost is content with the way his work has lasted.

Less happy is the terrifying spectre which has been seen steadily marching outside the castle walls. In 1927 a young guardsman on duty shot himself dead. Days later the comrades of the dead man saw his ghost slowly pacing along as if still on duty. The ghostly sentry has been seen many times since, continually treading the same guard route he had trod during his life.

A more pleasant spirit once roamed the palaces of the Rozmberk family in what is now Czechoslovakia. Flitting between the various homes of this aristocratic dynasty, the ghost became known as the White Lady of Bohemia. The spectre seemed to have an interest in the wellbeing of the family. On one occasion a nanny awoke in the middle of the night to find the White Lady cradling the infant heir of the Rozmberks in her arms. The White Lady gently laid the baby down and then vanished. Now that the Communist government has stripped noble families, such as the Rozmberks, of their power and wealth, the White Lady seems to have disappeared. She has not been seen in recent years.

A Warning from the Grave

In February 1682 an officer sleeping in Windsor Castle awoke to see the spirit of Sir George Villiers who had died some time earlier. The officer was told to take a message to the ghost's son, the Duke of Buckingham.

The ghost stated that the duke's life was in danger and that he needed to prepare for death. The Duke of Buckingham took the warning seriously. However, he was not able to avoid his fate. A few weeks later he was murdered.

The old Guard House, Windsor Castle. Many guards have reported supernatural activity near this spot.

Catching the Souls of the Dead

The most terrifying of all apparitions are those which come to call people to their graves. Once such a spirit is seen, death is inevitable. These fearful beings are found in all parts of the world. Though they take many guises and shapes, their purpose as harbingers of death is never in doubt.

Possibly the most dramatic and noisiest of these terrible beings are the banshees. Each banshee attaches itself to a particular family. Such families are usually the old noble Gaelic families of Ireland. When a member of the family is due to die, the banshee pays a visit.

The coming of the banshee is always a frightening and weird experience. The first manifestation of the banshee is usually a low moaning cry or a gentle sobbing. After several minutes this sound rises in volume and pitch to become a hideous scream of despair. The terrible sound then fades away to gentle sobbing. Sometimes the banshee will wail and cry for several days before death claims its victims. On other occasions only a single, horrific cry will be heard.

The banshee who utters the call is not seen as often as she is heard. But the few people who have gazed upon the banshee describe her as a beautiful young woman dressed in a long green dress and a grey shawl.

Perhaps the most famous man whose death was foretold by a banshee was King Brian Boru who died as he fought an army of Vikings in 1014.

But it is not only noble families who are visited by the banshee, nor is the spirit confined to Ireland. Banshees seem able to follow the family which they haunt across the world. Many less distinguished people are descended from ancient families. It can sometimes be surprising where the banshee wails.

James O'Barry, an American businessman of Irish descent, has heard the banshee wail twice, when his grandfather and father died. In 1979 a terrible wailing split the air at Winchester, England. A member of the McCormack family died almost at once. The banshee has even been seen in the middle of a battlefield. During the First World War a young man named Daniel O'Conner was serving in the British army in France. In 1915, the regiment was ordered forwards to attack a German position. The men scrambled out of the trench and were startled to see a banshee standing in their way. The banshee wailed and instantly German bullets killed Daniel O'Conner.

The Scottish counterpart of the banshee is known as the Washer at the Ford. This spirit appears as an old woman washing bloodstained clothes in a river or stream. The presence of the hideous old maid foretells the death of a relative or friend of the person who sees her.

The dim eerie rainforests of South America are said to be the home of visions as frightening as the banshee. Many of the Indians claim that the spirit Timakana has the power to bring death. Appearing as a man with burning red eyes and green skin, Timakana runs through the forest.

One Indian was camping deep in the jungle when Timakana walked out of the jungle and sat beside the fire. Shaking with fear, the Indian picked up a flaming branch from the fire and chased the spirit away. When the Indian turned back to the fire Timakana was again sitting beside the flames. The spirit looked at the

The banshee is an Irish spirit which comes to announce the approach of death.

Indian, smiled and walked away. Five days later the unfortunate Indian died.

A very similar phantom appears to bring death to members of the Ojibwa tribe in North America. This frightful being is the baykok. Appearing as a dreadfully thin man with glowing red eyes, the baykok hunts the souls of humans. The baykok can easily be frightened away, if it is seen. But if it manages to creep up on a sleeping Indian, the baykok cuts a small hole in its victim. Death inevitably follows.

The Ojibwa believe that spirits, such as the baykok, are dependant on water. During the winter, when lakes and rivers are frozen, the spirits are powerless. The baykok can only hunt during the warm months of summer.

A very different, but equally disconcerting bringer of death is to be found in Germany. This is the doppelgänger and many people have claimed to see this phantom immediately before their death. The frightening apparition takes the form of an exact double of the person who sees it.

Usually the doppelgänger first appears in an incomplete form. The person fated to die will catch a fleeting glimpse of the apparition several times without realizing what it is. Finally the victim will come face to face with their double and recognize it. Death is said to follow almost at once.

Herne the Hunter in his traditional dress of antlers and forest clothing.

Appointment in Samarra

Many Arabs believe that Death stalks the streets in the guise of a hideous woman. One man named Abdullah saw Death moving through the streets of Baghdad. Death did not see Abdullah. Hoping to escape Death, Abdullah leapt on to a horse and galloped out of Baghdad to stay with his family in Samarra. As the man galloped past, Death did notice him and stopped in surprise. A passing stranger asked Death why she looked so shocked. "Well" replied Death," I did not expect to see Abdullah in Baghdad. I have an appointment with him in Samarra."

Windsor Great Park, a favourite haunt of Herne the Hunter.

All these horrifying apparitions appear to proclaim coming death, but even after death has claimed a victim, the spirit world is not finished with the soul. Rushing through the countryside gallops the Wild Hunt, tracking down the souls of sinners.

The chief huntsman of this horrific collection of riders and hounds is often said to be Herne the Hunter. This strange figure always appears in his own peculiar set of clothes. Whenever Herne is seen he takes the form of a tall man in flowing robes. Strapped to the top of Herne's head is the skull of a deer with large antlers branching upwards.

The phantom apparitions of Herne the Hunter are sometimes seen in the Great Park of Windsor Castle. Local legend states that Herne is a ghost. It is said that Herne was a huntsman in the Great Park during the reign of Richard II in the late 14th century. Herne was so skilled at leading the king to fine kills, that the other huntsman became jealous. They plotted against Herne and caused him to commit suicide. The unhappy spirit of Herne then returned to haunt the Great Park.

Though there may well have been such a huntsman during the reign of Richard II, it is unlikely that Herne the Hunter is his ghost.

Herne appears in many places far from Windsor. He may be seen standing beneath a great oak or striding through forests, but his most dramatic appearance is as the leader of the Wild Hunt.

The few people who claim to have seen the Wild Hunt describe it as a grand and terrible spectacle. Astride a huge black horse, which breathes fire and whose feet spark lightning from the ground, Herne gallops through the night. Behind Herne ride a number of other horsemen dressed as normal huntsman. A pack of large hounds races ahead of the hunt, following the scent of the poor wretches who are fated to be their quarry. In some cases, the leader of the hunt is identified as the Devil, rather than Herne.

Many years ago a Duke of Richmond witnessed the Wild Hunt in full cry. He wrote "the low winding of a horn was heard. The sound was succeeded by the trampling of horses' hooves, and the next moment a vivid flash of lightning showed a troop of some 20 ghostly horsemen, headed by the demon hunter". The Wild Hunt is a truly terrifying sight.

It is possible that the Wild Hunt is somehow connected with the pagan religion once practised in England. The greatest god of the pagan

(Above) included among the folklore of the American cowboys was a ghost herd of wild demon cattle. Cowboys who lived a wicked life were thought to be damned to chase this herd for eternity. (Right) Woden, an ancient pagan god, rides out on his horse, Sleipnir, accompanied by his ravens and owl.

English was Woden. This god was believed to gallop across the world on his magical horse. When battles took place, the warriors believed that Woden sent out his handmaidens to collect the souls of the men who died bravely.

In later Viking myth the handmaidens of Woden were known as the Valkyries. These beautiful but violent women galloped through the night collecting souls. It is easy to see the connection between the Wild Hunt and Woden.

Death is a terrifying prospect which most people wish to avoid for as long as possible. It would not be surprising that human imagination, or superstition, has surrounded death with creatures such as banshees, baykok and the Wild Hunt. On the other hand, if any event should bring the world of man and the world of the spirits together it is death. Perhaps strange and savage beings do gather around at such fateful moments.

Halting the Wild Hunt

A farmer returning home across Dartmoor last century was met by the Wild Hunt as it galloped after fresh quarry. The man stopped the Master of the Hunt and asked if he had caught anything. "Aye," replied the huntsman. "Here's one for you." The huntsman threw a bundle of rags to the ground and galloped off. When the farmer inspected the rags, he found they contained the dead body of his own son.

TERROR ON THE HIGH SEAS

The Derelicts

On 5 December 1872 Captain David Morehouse was pacing the deck of his ship, the *Dei Gratia*, as it sailed across the Atlantic Ocean. Suddenly he spotted another ship some kilometres ahead of his own. Though Captain Morehouse did not know it, he had just become involved in one of the strangest and most puzzling mysteries of the sea.

As the *Dei Gratia* slowly overtook the other vessel, Captain Morehouse realized that something was wrong. He saw that the sails were torn to shreds and that the ship was rolling drunkenly in the sea. Morehouse hailed the ship, but there was no reply. Becoming concerned, Morehouse sent his mate, Deveau, and two men across in a rowboat.

As the men approached, they could read the name of the ship. She was the *Mary Celeste*. When Deveau and his men climbed aboard, they found a deserted ship. There was nobody on board. Only the gentle creaking of the rigging disturbed the silence. As the men searched the ship they became increasingly puzzled.

The ship's rowing boat was missing. The crew of the ship had clearly abandoned the *Mary Celeste*, but there was no reason why they should have done so. The ship was completely seaworthy and in no danger of sinking. Below

Captain David Morehouse, master of the Dei Gratia, *who discovered the abandoned* Mary Celeste.

deck the cabins were tidy and neat. In one cabin a sheet of music still rested on a melodeon. Unsure of what to do with the *Mary Celeste*, Morehouse put a prize crew on board and sailed both ships to Gibraltar.

Here an official enquiry was set up to discover the fate of the crew of the *Mary Celeste*. Investigations soon revealed much about the voyage of the ship. She had left New York under the command of Captain Benjamin Briggs, an experienced seaman. On board was a full crew and Briggs' wife and child. The cargo had been one of barrels of alcohol.

The logbook of the *Mary Celeste* was read for clues. The voyage appeared to have been perfectly normal up to and including 25 November, when the last entry was made. One of the barrels of alcohol had been broken open and an old sword lay in a cabin. At first the sword was thought to be bloodstained, but the marks turned out to be rust.

It was suggested at the inquiry that the crews

of the *Dei Gratia* and *Mary Celeste* had collaborated to claim the insurance money on the ship. However, this could not be proved. Other suggestions were made. Some people thought that the crew had become drunk on the opened barrel of alcohol and murdered Captain Briggs. They might then have fled the ship in the boat. Alternative suggestions were that Briggs had gone mad and driven his men to mutiny. However, no theory made sense and the inquiry returned an open verdict.

In the years since the *Mary Celeste* was found many fresh ideas have been put forward to explain the disappearance of her crew. However, nobody has ever really solved the puzzle. The fate which overtook an entire crew and left no trace either of them or itself must have been swift and lethal indeed.

Twenty-eight years after the affair of the *Mary Celeste*, the Atlantic Ocean swallowed more men without trace. This time the scene of the disappearance was a lighthouse on the isolated Flannan Islands, off the west coast of Scotland.

On 26 December 1900, Joseph Moore, a relief lighthouse keeper, arrived at the Flannan Island Lighthouse. The three men who should have been manning the lighthouse were not there. Only two clues to the fate of the men were found. First, two sets of oil skins were missing and, secondly, the last date in the record book was for 15 December.

At first it was thought that the three men had been washed out to sea by a large wave. But weather records showed that no storm had occurred on the 15 December. Even if a freak wave were responsible for the disappearance, it is unlikely that all three men would have perished together.

Puzzling and disconcerting as these disappearances are, they lack the sheer horror of the fate which overtook the crew of the *Marlborough* in 1890. In January of that year the ship left New Zealand with a cargo of sheep and set sail for England. When the *Marlborough* did not arrive, it was assumed that she had been wrecked during a storm.

Twenty-three years later, the *Marlborough* was found. The crew of the *Johnston* found the

Captain Morehouse hailed the strange ship, but there was no reply.

missing ship drifting aimlessly in the South Atlantic Ocean. As the two ships neared each other, the sides, decks and masts of the *Marlborough* were seen to be green with mold and moss and the rigging was rotting away.

On the decks of the *Marlborough* there was an horrific sight. Dozens of skeletons were scattered around. All of the skeletons were lying as if the men had died suddenly while on duty. It was clear that whatever had killed the crew had struck swiftly. No known disease can kill a whole crew so quickly that none lives long enough to bury the others. Equally surprising was the fact that the ship had drifted around the world for so many years without being seen. Nobody could account for the strange fate of the *Marlborough*.

Forever Sailing

It is not only people who return from the dead. The phantoms of inanimate objects are often seen many years after they have been destroyed. Of these possibly the most unnerving are the ghost ships which roam the oceans. The lonely sailor catching sight of one of these horrific spirits far from land could well be forgiven for being struck dumb with terror.

Possibly the most famous phantom ship is the sailing vessel known as the Flying Dutchman. This ghost has been sighted several times in the past three centuries. Every time the Flying Dutchman is seen, a remarkably similar description is given. The ship appears to be a large merchantman of the 17th century. Whatever the weather at the time of the sighting, the Flying Dutchman appears to be battling through raging storms.

According to the story told about this dreadful ship, it is the fearful vessel captained by the Dutch sea captain Vanderdecken. One day in the middle of the 17th century, Vanderdecken put to sea heading for the Far East. With a valuable cargo aboard, the ship sailed peacefully across the Atlantic Ocean until it reached Cape Horn.

A fearful storm struck as the ship tried to round Cape Horn. For days on end the ship battled against the storm. Sails were torn to ribbons and masts torn away. The crew begged Vanderdecken to put into a safe port, but the captain refused. He laughed and blasphemously swore he would carry on sailing until he rounded the Horn. At that moment a strange figure appeared on the deck. The figure, who some say was God, condemned Vanderdecken for his pride telling him to sail the seas until the end of time.

These are the traditional origins of the Flying Dutchman. Though it seems an unlikely tale, many people swear to have seen the phantom ship. One of the most distinguished witnesses was Prince George, later King George V. He sighted the ghost, along with 13 other men, on 11 June 1881, off the coast of Australia.

Other phantom ships are less famous than the Flying Dutchman, but are just as likely to be seen. In the 1890s the steamer *SS Violet* was wrecked on the Goodwin Sands in the English Channel and everybody on board was drowned. On several occasions, seamen on ships near the Goodwin Sands have seen the phantom of this Victorian steamer piling on to the sand banks and being torn to pieces by the waves. It has even been claimed that the screams of the dying can be heard. One such witness alerted the coastguards, believing that he had seen a real wreck. A full scale search was mounted but, needless to say, no ship was found.

Steer to the North East

Sent to the captain's cabin on an errand, a sailor froze when he opened the door. Writing something in the log was a man he had never seen on the ship before. As the sailor watched the stranger faded into nothingness. But written in the log were the words "Steer to the north east." The captain of the ship did so and came across a sinking ship. He took the survivors aboard. One of the men from the striken vessel was identical with the figure seen hours earlier in the captain's cabin.

Battling forever against stormy seas, the Flying Dutchman is a famous phantom ship.

The Cursed Ships

There are several ships which have acquired reputations for being unlucky. Numerous accidents happen to these ships and bad fortune seems to follow them. Though there is no reason for certain ships to be cursed or jinxed, the belief that some are is widespread.

The German submarine UB65 earned a terrible reputation among German sailors during the First World War. A fame which was to continue from the time she was built until her end.

Work began on the UB65 in the summer of 1916, one of 24 submarines destined to aid Germany's war effort. A week later, a falling girder killed two men working on the ship. When she was nearly complete, the UB65 suddenly filled with poisonous fumes from her engines. Three more men died.

The deaths continued to take place aboard the U-boat. During her trials a man was swept overboard and drowned. When the craft was

taking on provisions after her maiden voyage a torpedo exploded killing four men and the second officer.

A few weeks later, the UB65 was due to return to sea. One of two men on watch on deck suddenly ran below gibbering with fright. When the officers climbed on deck, they found the second lookout cowering behind the conning tower in terror. Both men had seen the ghost of the dead second officer striding aboard.

On many occasions on the following voyage the phantom officer was seen. On 21 January 1918, the lookout and captain both saw the ghost standing on the deck, staring up at the conning tower. Large waves washed across the deck, but the ghost remained unmoved. By the time the U-boat returned from this voyage the crew and officers were seriously demoralized. They were convinced that the haunted U-boat was condemned to a hideous end. Almost to a man, they requested transfer to other ships.

With a new crew, the UB65 put to sea again in May 1918. For some time the jinx seemed to

have left her. But then the ghostly officer was seen again. A few days later a sailor became mad and threw himself overboard. The phantom was being seen more and more often. On 10 July the UB65 was sighted off Cape Clear by the American vessel L2. As the Americans prepared to open fire, the UB65 exploded. The blast was staggering in size and stunned the Americans.

No explanation has ever been found for the mysterious blast which destroyed the UB65. But before she sailed on her last voyage, several seamen on board had been convinced they would not return. Perhaps the jinx had finally claimed the U-boat.

Another ship which seemed to be dogged by bad luck was the *Great Republic*. This great American sailing ship was launched on 4 October 1853. Many old sailors who watched the ceremony were filled with foreboding. Instead of wine, the ship was launched with a bottle of water because of the influence of the local temperance league.

The ghostly second officer of UB65 was often seen by members of the crew, stalking through the submarine. The captain of the ship first saw the spectre on deck as waves broke over him.

Within weeks of launching, the *Great Republic* was reduced almost to a wreck by a devastating fire. She was rebuilt and sent to sea. Soon a succession of accidents gave the ship the reputation of being unlucky. On one particularly ominous occasion, a sailor died of an unknown disease. The burial service was read by the captain and the man's body tipped overboard. Immediately a freak wave washed the corpse back on board.

The ship eventually foundered for no apparent cause after 19 years of bad luck and fatal accidents. Such a succession of misfortunes could be explained away as mere coincidence. However, many people, particularly those who spend their lives at sea, firmly believe that certain ships are jinxed and are followed by bad luck.

SECRET ROOMS AND SKELETONS

Ghosts and Hidden Chambers

Many ghosts seem to be attached to rooms which have been blocked up and forgotten. When the hidden chambers are found once more, the spirits of the dead leave and the hauntings cease.

In the 1930s a couple named Ewings moved to Lynton, Devon, and rented one of the oldest houses in the town. Almost at once the Ewings realized that the house was haunted. The sound of a child crying could be heard in the scullery. When the Ewings' young nephew came to stay he was given the bedroom above the scullery. After just one night the boy refused to sleep in the room again. He said that there was a "nasty lady" there.

After several months of disturbances, Mr Ewings' brother came to stay. He noticed something which the Ewings had not. The bedroom above the scullery was smaller than the room below. On investigating the bedroom, a walled off cupboard was found. Inside the

cupboard was a child's box, a dead bat and some human bones.

The bones were taken to a doctor who passed them on to the police. It appeared that they were the remains of a young child. The sound of a child crying ceased at once. However, the spirit of the woman lingered for a while. Mrs Ewing saw the ghost several months later.

Careful investigation into the history of the house revealed that it had once been a home for the children of parents too poor to bring them up. One of the children had disappeared in mysterious circumstances. Perhaps the house had been the scene of a tragedy, the secret of which lay hidden in the blocked cupboard.

Less suspicious is the story behind the hidden room of Mrs Penn. In 1538 Mrs Sibell Penn was placed in charge of the young Prince Edward, son of Henry VIII. Mrs Penn quickly grew to love the boy and treated him well. When Edward became king in 1547 at the age of nine, Mrs Penn became one of the most favoured ladies at court.

However, following the early death of Edward in 1553, Mrs Penn virtually retired from court. She was given a suite of rooms at Hampton Court and lived quietly until her

Several phantoms seem particularly attached to rooms and cupboards which have been blocked up. Perhaps some terrible secret lies hidden in the chambers which the ghosts cannot forget.

death in 1562. Her rooms were then refurbished and another tenant moved in.

Before long, strange sounds began to be heard in the rooms. Most of the people who heard these strange sounds agreed that they resembled the noise made by a spinning wheel. The spinning wheel was not heard often, but the noise was quite distinct. Then the ghost of Mrs Penn appeared. Dressed in a long robe and a small hat, Mrs Penn's spirit was seen walking quietly through her old home.

The ghostly disturbances continued for many years, until it was decided to refurbish the rooms once again. Behind some panelling was found a door. This led to a small entirely forgotten room. Within the room, workmen were staggered to find a spinning wheel. The boards beneath the wheel were worn, as if the wheel was in continuous use, yet nobody had entered the room since the death of Mrs Penn.

The sounds of the spinning wheel ceased as soon as the hidden room was discovered, but the ghost of Mrs Penn is still seen occasionally.

Another ghost connected with a hidden chamber is still said to be active. Three centuries ago Lady Ferrers of Markyate, Hertfordshire, took to the life of a highwaywoman in search of excitement. After a successful criminal career lasting several years, Lady Ferrers was shot and killed. Her secret hoard of treasure has never been found. To this day the ghost of Lady Ferrers rides around the countryside. Perhaps, if the treasure ever is found, the ghost of Lady Ferrers might cease its haunting.

The Ghost and the Books

In the 1880s a house in St Anne's Street, Chester, was plagued by a ghost. On many evenings, heavy footsteps were heard climbing the stairs, though nobody could be seen. The ghost reached the landing and then stopped. One evening, as the family sat around the fire, a number of old books tumbled down from the chimney. Before they could be saved, the books burnt completely. Following the destruction of the books, the ghost was never heard again.

The Horror of Glamis

Nobody outside the Strathmore family knows the true nature of the horror of Glamis. Whatever that horror really is, it has exerted a strong hold over the noble family of the Earl of Strathmore and Kinghorne. According to tradition the heir to Strathmore is told the terrible secret on his 21st birthday. At least one happy young man has been transformed into a morose character by the gloomy information.

The earliest tale of a secret room at Glamis dates back to the time of Charles, sixth Earl of Strathmore and Kinghorne who died in 1728. This earl was very fond of gambling with cards. Many evenings passed at Glamis while the earl played cards with his neighbours, tenants or anyone else he could tempt into a game. So compulsive was the urge to gamble, that the earl would even play for pennies with kitchen servants.

One particular evening, the earl invited his neighbours, the Lindays, and a friend, James Carnegie, round for dinner. After a magnificent meal and some heavy drinking, the gentlemen retired to the earl's gaming room and gambling began. The amounts of money being wagered rose very high, until they reached a point where the Lindsays refused to play any further.

The sixth Earl had lost a great deal of money and he became very angry. While in a foul temper, the earl accused James Carnegie of cheating. In that period, when a man put his honour above all else, such an accusation meant that a duel was inevitable. Carnegie ran the earl through the body with his sword and killed him.

The sixth Earl was buried with all the honour due to his station and the seventh Earl took up residence in Glamis. However, the spirit of the sixth Earl did not rest easy in its grave. Within a few days of the fatal game of cards, the sound of voices was heard coming from the gambling room. Every evening a game of cards was played by the ghost of the sixth Earl. The sound of his voice, quarrelling with his gaming partners and shouting out bets, became insufferable.

Glamis Castle.

The seventh Earl had the room bricked up and forgotten about.

It is in this story that a hidden chamber at Glamis is first mentioned, but the true horror of Glamis belongs to a later generation. This tale, too, involves a secret room.

Early in the 19th century tales began to circulate that the Earl of Strathmore and Kinghorne had a terrible secret, which he kept locked in a secret room at Glamis. As the rumours of a dreadful mystery spread, a friend asked the then earl what the secret was. The earl turned to his friend and declared, "If you could guess the nature of this secret, you would go down on your knees and thank God that it were not yours."

At about the same time, the Earl of Strathmore and Kinghorne built a new wing at Glamis. He instructed the servants and his children that they must never again sleep in the old part of the house, but were to live within the new wing.

A few years later, in 1877, the Bishop of Brechin, an old friend of the earl, noticed that the nobleman was becoming increasingly sad. He asked the earl if there was anything which he, as a clergyman, could do to help. The earl thanked his friend but declared that nobody could help him.

On one occasion, this same earl invited some friends to stay for a few days. While the house party was in progress, the earl was called away on business. The guests decided to take advantage of his absence to search for the secret room. They visited every room they could find and draped a towel out of the window. When this was done, the guests filed outside to see if any windows had not been marked.

To their surprise, no less than a dozen windows visible outside had not been marked from the inside. The guests were about to return indoors and search for the missed rooms when the earl returned. He realized what was going on and flew into a terrible temper. His friends left the house in disgrace.

From such evidence as this, many people concluded that there was indeed some secret hidden at Glamis. The most popular explanation of the mystery concerned a hideous birth. It was said that early in the 19th century Lady Strathmore gave birth to a long awaited son and heir. But the baby was so hideously malformed that it was hidden away. The word was spread that the child had died at birth.

As the years passed, more sons were born, but the true heir lived on in a secret room deep in the castle. The existence of this misshapen monster was the secret revealed to each heir on his 21st birthday, for the hidden son was the true earl. A variation of this tale states that such a monster is born to each generation of the family.

The Famous Resident of Glamis

Perhaps the best-known member of the family which owns Glamis Castle is the Queen Mother. She was born in 1900 and spent many years of her childhood at Glamis Castle. During the First World War, the future Queen Mother acted as a nurse to the many wounded soldiers cared for at Glamis. She married the future King George VI in 1923.

A less popular theory to explain the horror of Glamis again concerns a hidden room. This tale states that, centuries ago, when clan warfare was common in the area, a band of Ogilvies came to Glamis. They were being hunted by the clan Lindsay and begged the earl to shelter them.

The then earl was an enemy of both the Ogilvies and the Lindsays. He invited the Ogilvies in and hid them in a secret chamber. The Lindsays passed by, but the earl did not release the Ogilvies. He left them in the secret room to starve to death. According to this tale, the secret room at Glamis contains the skeletons of the wretched Ogilvies who died at the hands of the earl.

Glamis Castle is now open to the public and anyone who wishes may visit the site of the mysterious horror. The guides who show visitors round the castle are well aware of the stories and legends which have gathered around Glamis, and they quite willingly show a secret room to visitors. This particular hidden chamber has been known for years. It was probably constructed as a hiding place for valuables or for important documents.

If there is a secret room at Glamis containing a terrible horror, the helpful guides do not show it to the paying public.

The Scottish Monster

The Scottish castle of The Hermitage, south of Edinburgh, is haunted by a "monster" from the past. Lord Soulis was a black magician and murderer who was eventually killed by local villagers. His ghost still haunts the castle.

The secret room at Chambercombe Manor, Ilfracombe, North Devon, can still be seen today. This room lay hidden for nearly 300 years.

Hidden Skeletons

In the early 19th century a farmer living in Chambercombe Manor, Devon, decided to make some repairs to the house roof. As he climbed a ladder to the roof, the farmer noticed some loose plaster on the wall. Scraping it away, he found a bricked up window. The innocent farmer had stumbled upon a grisly secret some three centuries old.

The farmer realized that the blocked window was not visible from inside the house, which indicated that a secret room lay within Chambercombe Manor. He hurried indoors and, with the help of some workmen, broke into a hidden chamber. He was surprised to find that the room was fully furnished with chairs, tapestries and a four-poster bed. The farmer stepped forwards through the dust and drew back the curtains of the bed. What he saw caused him to leap backwards with a cry of horror. On the bed lay a gleaming skeleton.

This discovery was horrific enough, but the story behind it is one of tragedy and disaster. It appears that about 300 years earlier Chambercombe Manor had been rented by a man named Alexander Oatway. Oatway was a leader of a gang of wreckers. These men would go down to the coast during the height of a storm and erect lights. In turn, these tempted storm-battered ships to head for the land, thinking they had found a safe anchorage. Instead, they would crash into the rocks and were destroyed. Then the wreckers would plunder the ship and savagely kill anyone who survived.

On one such expedition, Oatway's son, William, rescued a beautiful young woman from the sea. The couple later married and moved to

Oatway had died and Chambercombe Manor had new tenants.

Years passed and William Oatway felt he would like to return to Chambercombe Manor, his boyhood home. When Oatway learnt that

Lundy Island. They had a daughter named Katherine who married an Irish sea captain and moved to Dublin. By this time Alexander

William Oatway heard a cry for help and found a badly injured young woman.

the house was empty and needed tenants, he moved there with his wife.

Some time later a ship was driven ashore and wrecked near Chambercombe during a storm. William Oatway ran down to the beach to find out if he could help any of the unfortunates who had been on board the ship. Only one body showed any signs of life. It was of a young woman who had terrible head injuries.

William Oatway carried the injured woman back to Chambercombe Manor, but despite all efforts, she died. As William and his wife prepared the body for burial, they noticed a richly jewelled belt strapped around the dead woman's waist. The golden belt was worth a

fortune. The temptation proved too much for Oatway. He removed the belt determined to sell it for cash.

Oatway realized that if anyone knew that he had brought the woman's body from the wreck, they would ask for the jewelled belt. So Oatway blocked off the room in which the unfortunate woman lay and plastered over the window.

A few days later an official arrived asking if Oatway knew anything about the wreck as one passenger was still unaccounted for. Sticking to his plan, Oatway denied all knowledge of the woman's fate. The officials next words struck horror into the heart of William Oatway.

The missing passenger was Oatway's own daughter, Katherine. The injuries sustained by the woman had so disfigured her face that Oatway had not recognized her. Realizing that he had robbed the corpse of his own daughter, and that her skeleton was hidden in the house, Oatway fled from Chambercombe. He never returned.

To this day, the ghost of a pretty young woman glides through the rooms of Chambercombe Manor. Some think that it is the spirit of young Katherine Oatway. Others maintain that it is the ghost of Lady Jane Grey, who stayed in Chambercombe for some years, and was later beheaded. Whatever the truth, the ghost is seen frequently and, since Chambercombe Manor is

now open to the public, innocent visitors are among the many witnesses.

Unlike the spirit of Katherine Oatway, many ghosts disappear once their skeletons are found and given a proper burial. The oldest example of this happened in Athens, Greece, 2,000 years ago. A fine villa in the city was haunted by the horrific ghost of an old man fettered by iron chains. Noticing that the spectre usually vanished at a particular spot, the tenant of the villa dug into the ground. He found a skeleton bound by

The staircase at Chambercombe Manor.

rusty chains. The body was buried properly and the ghost walked no more.

Less frightening were the two ghosts who used to be seen in Fountain Court at Hampton Court. Dressed as dashing young cavaliers of the 17th century, the phantom pair were often seen strolling across the lawns. The ghosts, one of whom was described as being handsome,

The charming exterior of Chambercombe Manor.

seemed to be chatting together quite contentedly.

One day workmen digging in the court came across two skeletons buried a few feet below the ground. The bones were removed and given a proper burial. The ghosts were never seen again. Subsequent research showed that two young cavaliers had been killed near Hampton Court during the English Civil War. One, Lord Francis Villiers, was said to be extremely handsome. Perhaps the skeletons belonged to these two brave young men.

More vicious was the spirit which haunted Hylton Castle in County Durham. In 1609 the lord of the castle, Sir Robert Hylton, killed his stable boy, Robert Skelton, in a fit of temper and threw the body into a pond. Soon afterwards the ghost of the boy returned. The spirit quickly earned the name of the Cold Lad of Hylton.

The activity of this ghost became legendary. Furniture was thrown around the castle, loud crashes rang out at the dead of night and trees would be shaken from side to side when there was no wind. The centre of these terrifying activities was the bedroom of Robert Skelton, which few people dared to enter.

In 1703, the pond into which Sir Robert had thrown his victim was drained. The skeleton of the Cold Lad was found and given proper burial. Soon afterwards the last of the Hylton family died without an heir and the Cold Lad was seen no more.

A similarly vengeful ghost used to haunt the Marquis of Granby pub near Esher, Surrey. Many years ago a young serving girl accidently locked herself in an upstairs cupboard. She starved to death before anybody could find her. The troubled spirit of the wretched girl used to stalk the pub causing all types of trouble. But when a large family Bible was propped against the cupboard door, the ghost stayed quiet. The Bible remains there to this day.

The phantom cavaliers of Hampton Court were never seen after a pair of skeletons were discovered and given a Christian burial.

Screaming Skulls

For some reason many souls seem particularly attached to the skulls which they inhabited when alive. This has sometimes caused great trouble for the living left behind. The most famous and terrifying manifestation of this type of haunting are the screaming skulls which lie in many English country houses.

One of the most famous of these sinister bones is to be found in a cardboard box in Bettiscombe Manor in Dorset. The origins of the skull are obscure, but nobody doubts the power which it holds over the household. The present owner dare not allow the skull out of the house and people are not encouraged to gaze upon the gruesome object.

The most popular theory regarding the origin of the skull concerns a man named Azariah Pinney, son of the owner of Bettiscombe Manor. Azariah joined the rebellion of the Duke of Monmouth in 1685 and was exiled to the West Indies.

Azariah founded a business in the West Indies and became a wealthy man. John Pinney, Azariah's grandson, eventually returned to Bettiscombe, bringing with him a black slave. As the slave lay dying he swore that he would never rest unless his body was buried in his far homeland. John, however, refused to pay for such an expensive burial and had the slave interred at the local church.

The screaming began almost at once. The yells echoed around the churchyard every night. At Bettiscombe Manor ghostly hands slammed doors and rattled windows. Local residents finally forced John Pinney to dig up the slave's body and ship it back to the West Indies. The skull from the slave, however, was removed and kept at Bettiscombe. Another version of the tale states that the skull was excavated from a prehistoric graveyard near to the house.

However the skull came to Bettiscombe, it was certainly there in the early part of the last century. The man who then owned the manor found the skull particularly irritating. He decided to get rid of the grisly relic by throwing it into a pond in the grounds. As the man retired to bed a dreadful scream shattered the silence.

Leaping from their beds, the inhabitants of the manor tried to find the source of the scream. They thought that somebody might be in trouble. They could find nobody and the screaming died away.

The next evening the dreadful screaming broke out again. It rang through the house and echoed along corridors. Thoroughly unnerved by the heart-rending cries, the owner of Bettiscombe waded into his pond and retrieved the

terrible skull. It has not been moved outside the house since.

Similar unearthly screams ring through the rooms of Berkeley Castle, though little mystery surrounds the ghostly origins of these disturbing noises. In 1327 King Edward II was deposed by his wife, Queen Isabelle, and her lover, Sir Roger Mortimer. The unfortunate king was then imprisoned at Berkeley Castle. At first the king's imprisonment was fairly agreeable. He

Berkeley Castle, Gloucestershire,
was the prison of King Edward II. He was held in
this room (below) and then the dungeon (above).

was held in a large comfortable room and had plenty to eat.

However, many people felt that Edward should rule England rather than Queen Isabelle. The queen therefore sent orders that Edward should be killed. She hoped that this would make her hold on the throne more secure. First, the jailers at Berkeley threw King Edward into a dank dungeon. They hoped that he would catch a disease and die naturally. But Edward remained healthy. On the night of 21 September 1327, the men holding King Edward murdered him. The screams of the dying king echoed through the castle and woke up several villagers living nearby.

The terrible cries of King Edward are sometimes heard echoing around Berkeley Castle even to the present day. The agonizing screams are said to disturb everyone who hears them.

Less violent in origin, but equally terrifying are the screams which boom around Burton Agnes Hall in Humberside. The building was constructed in the 17th century by three sisters, the daughters of Sir Henry Griffith. Of the three, the most enthusiastic builder was the youngest, Anne. She took a great interest in the design of the house and the materials to be used.

Soon after the completion of Burton Agnes Hall, Anne Griffith was attacked by robbers. She was rescued and carried home to the hall, but it was soon clear that Anne was dying. As life slipped away, Anne asked her sisters to cut off her head and keep it in Burton Agnes Hall. The two sisters, however, did not do as they had promised but buried Anne in the churchyard.

Exactly one week later the peace of Burton Agnes Hall was shattered in a terrible way. In the dead of night, a door in the hall slammed shut with a loud crash. Footsteps were heard running along the corridors. Then a fearsome, piercing scream rang out. A servant boy leapt from his bed armed with a dagger and ran through the house. He could find no cause for the noises. A week afterwards exactly the same sounds woke the household in terror. After a third week of horror, the sisters visited the vicar.

On his advice, the grave of Anne Griffith was opened. Though her body had not yet decayed, the skull was gleaming white and separate from

the body. Hoping to escape the terrible nocturnal noises, the Griffith sisters carried Anne's skull to Burton Agnes Hall. The supernatural trouble ceased at once.

Many years later, however, new residents came to Burton Agnes Hall. They found the presence of the grinning skull disconcerting. The grisly relic was removed from the house and buried. That very night loud crashes, running footsteps and eerie screams rang through Burton Agnes Hall. The skull was excavated and returned to the hall. It has not been removed since.

The magnificent Jacobean decoration of the Great Hall at Burton Agnes.

More terrible in their thirst for revenge were the screaming skulls of Calgarth. Their story is a frightening example of vengeance from beyond the grave. In the early 17th century the site of Calgarth was occupied by a small farm owned by Kraster and Dorothy Cook. Myles Phillipson, the local magistrate and a rich landowner, wished to build his manor house at Calgarth, but the Cooks refused to sell the land.

Determined to gain the site by fair means or

The Floating Head

In Dundee stands an old house, which was once a hotel. Several guests staying in a particular room complained of a disturbing ghost which appeared at the dead of night. The apparition took the form of a disembodied head which glowed in the darkness. Emerging from a cupboard the head drifted around the room for some time before descending through the floor. An 18th century pedlar had been murdered in the room and his head hidden in the cupboard.

foul, Phillipson invited the Cooks to Christmas dinner. During the meal, Myles Phillipson hid a valuable gold bowl in the Cooks' belongings. He then accused the innocent couple of theft and had them arrested. In those days, theft of such a valuable object was punishable by death. In the subsequent trial, the Cooks were found guilty and dragged off for execution. As she was hauled from the court, Dorothy Cook cursed Myles Phillipson and the house he wanted to build on the Cooks' farm.

By the following Christmas, Calgarth Hall was complete and Myles Phillipson and his family had taken up residence. The Phillipsons invited all their neighbours to spend Christmas with them in the fine new house. It was an invitation all present soon wished they had not accepted. As the party sat down to dinner, a large joint of roast beef was brought forwards.

Suddenly, a high pitched scream rang through the building. Scream followed scream in a series of heart-chilling yells. One guest, braver than the others, grabbed his rapier and dashed into the hallway to discover the source of the cries. Lying on the staircase were two gleaming skulls.

Thinking he was the victim of some horrible joke, Phillipson threw the skulls out of the window. Later he and his guests retired to bed. At two o'clock the terrible screams echoed around Calgarth Hall once more. Phillipson tumbled from his bed and ran on to the landing, to find the skulls back on the staircase.

In the following months it became clear that the gruesome skulls could not be disposed of. Any attempt to remove them precipitated fresh outbursts of unearthly screaming. More ominous, the skulls always returned. Within a few months, bad luck began to haunt Myles Phillipson. His business lost money at an alarming rate, he became almost continually ill and every venture in which he had a stake failed.

Eventually, Myles Phillipson died almost in poverty. The only remnant of his once-vast wealth which he left his son was Calgarth Hall. On the night of Myles Phillipson's death, the skulls screamed for hours on end. Peace only came with the dawn. After this noisy outburst, the skulls became quieter. Each year their

activity lessened. But for generations the skulls would scream on Christmas day or if they were removed from Calgarth Hall.

More active in revenge even than the skulls of Calgarth was the severed head of Melbrigith, Earl of Caithness. In the middle of the 11th century, Melbrigith was fighting a bitter feud with Sigurd, Earl of Orkney. The feud reached its climax in a great battle during which Melbrigith was wounded. Sigurd approached the dying earl to gloat over his victory. Melbrigith gazed proudly at Sigurd and cursed him as life ebbed away.

Sigurd took no notice of the dying man's curse. He simply bent forwards and hacked off Melbrigith's head. Lifting his grisly trophy, Sigurd laughed and tied it to his saddle. With victory won, Earl Sigurd and his men rode home. The triumphant warriors trotted along, and the head of Melbrigith knocked against the saddle of Sigurd.

As the riders crossed a patch of rough ground, the severed head bounced high and twisted round. Then the head fell, its jaws were gaping and struck against Sigurd's leg. The jagged teeth of Melbrigith bit deep into Sigurd's flesh, bringing blood gushing from the leg. The earl yelled in pain and fell from his horse. The savage wound quickly became infected and turned gangrenous. Within three days Sigurd died. He had been killed by the severed head of his old enemy.

The Celtic Cult

The Celtic people who inhabited the British Isles before the Roman Invasion of AD 43 were pagans who worshipped many gods. One of the most widespread cults of the time was that of the severed head. Skulls were placed on altars and prisoners of war sacrificed by decapitation. The heads of great men were believed to contain magical powers. On many occasions skulls of relatives or enemies would be preserved in a house for years. Perhaps this is the origin of the practice of keeping skulls in houses.

The savage Sigurd, Earl of Orkney, was killed by a bite from the severed head of his old enemy.

HOUSES OF TERROR

The Demon Drummer

The horrific story of the demon drummer began quite mundanely when a beggar was hauled before a magistrate by the name of Mompesson in March 1661. The beggar was well-known in the district for playing a drum. He was found guilty of a minor crime and sent to jail. Mompesson confiscated the drum and took it home to Tedworth House, Wiltshire. The ghostly trouble began three nights later.

As the Mompesson family lay asleep, a terrific hammering noise woke them up. It sounded as if somebody was kicking the doors in the house. Though Mr Mompesson searched the building no intruder could be found. The next night the door-thumping occurred again. A few nights later, the banging noises echoed along a corridor and into the room where the beggar's drum was kept. There was a moment's silence. Then the drum began to play. A long roll sounded out and after that silence returned.

The next night the drum played again. As the days passed, the drum became more and more active. It floated through the air and played itself

for long periods of time. While the drum played, other terrifying phenomenon frightened the family. Shoes and chairs were hurled across rooms. Floorboards were ripped up and the children had their hair pulled by invisible hands. On one occasion, the demon drummer became visible for a time. Its glowing red eyes scared a servant so much that he left the house immediately and never returned.

After several weeks of these upsetting phenomena, Mr Mompesson received a message from the beggar, who was now free from jail. The beggar demanded the return of his drum, saying that he was responsible for the disturbances. Far from returning the drum, Mompesson promptly rearrested the man and charged him with

witchcraft. The begger was found guilty and transported to America. The dreadful drumming then suddenly stopped.

The Drum of Death

The family of the Scottish Earls of Airlie is said to be haunted by a phantom drummer. The spectral figure, more often heard than seen, appears to play a drumroll whenever a member of the family dies. It is said that the demon drummer is the ghost of a drummerboy sent as a messenger to a previous Earl of Airlie by an enemy clan. The earl killed the drummer boy and stuffed him inside his own drum as an answer to the message.

The Modern Boggart

In past centuries, country families in Britain believed that certain mischievous spirits might attach themselves to a house. These invisible beings were thought to delight in causing trouble. They slammed doors, threw furniture around and hammered on walls. The spirits were known as boggarts and were thought to be evil fairies. Of course, tales about wicked fairies are not usually believed in this century and the boggarts ceased to be thought of as real beings.

However, strange and frightening events in recent years have brought the boggarts back into the news. They are now usually referred to by their German name of poltergeist, which means "noisy ghost".

Some poltergeists create only minor disturbances. Small objects may be missing for several days to turn up in a place where they are never normally kept. A few loud thumps might also be heard. However, the truly active poltergeist is a terrifying phenomenon. Some of these hauntings have been subjected to scientific inquiry. However, no adequate explanation of the events has been put forward.

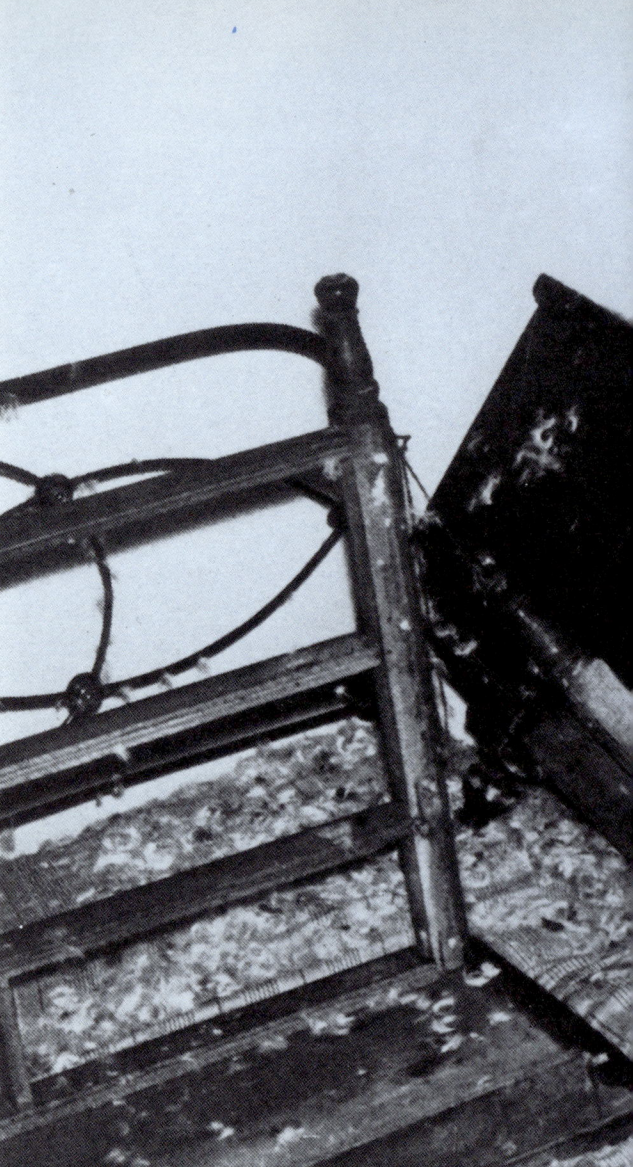

Fleeing the Boggart

Late last century, the Yorkshire farm of George Gilbertson was plagued by a boggart. After several months disturbed by slamming doors, thrown shoes and loud crashes, George Gilbertson decided to take his family away from the haunted home. The furniture was loaded on to a cart and the family left. As the cart rumbled through the village a friend stopped George and asked why he was leaving.

"Well," replied George, "it's that boggart. He's got so noisy we've got to go."

At that moment a loud bang sounded from inside a cupboard and the boggart shouted out, "Aye, we're all leaving you see!"

George Gilbertson sighed sadly and turned back to his old home. There could be no escape from the boggart.

In the French town of Mulhouse, an extremely vicious poltergeist haunted a family for many months in the early 1980s. The troublesome spirit seemed to enjoy playing the tricks common to other poltergeists: books were moved around on bookshelves so that they were out of order, ornaments were thrown about and a table was once seen to dance across a room on its own. However, unlike most other poltergeists, this spirit seemed intent on injuring the mother of the family. On several occasions the woman felt as if she had been punched by invisible fists. She was dragged from her bed at night and was even badly cut. Despite serious investigations by scientists, no logical explanation for the events could be found.

Less destructive was the poltergeist which

Some of the damage caused by the poltergeist which harassed the Glynn family in Runcorn, Cheshire, in 1952.

plagued a family in Enfield, London, during the 1970s. The uncanny activities began in September 1977, when the sound of footsteps was heard in a bedroom. Within a few days, the poltergeist became extremely active. A hairbrush was thrown and hit one member of the family on the head and a heavy bed dragged across a floor. When a policewoman entered the house, a chair was thrown across the room. During the night, bedclothes were torn from sleeping members of the family. Such disturbances are typical of poltergeist activity, they are irritating and frightening, but rarely truly dangerous. The activities continued for three years and then abruptly stopped.

Many investigators of the paranormal have studied poltergeists and tried to explain them.

Some experts think that the frightening activities are unconsciously controlled by a member of the haunted household. Often the poltergeist is only active when one particular person is present. However, others think that this is due to the fact that an evil spirit has become attached to that person. A few investigators consider poltergeists to be nothing but trickery by children wanting to gain attention.

However, nobody really knows the truth behind poltergeist activity. Perhaps the wicked fairies known as boggarts do exist and delight in causing trouble.

The Most Haunted House in England?

On the night of 27 February 1939, the abandoned rectory at Borley, Essex, erupted in flames. The fire spread rapidly through the old house. Villagers rushed to the scene, but could do little except watch the progress of the flames. Although the building had been empty for years, many villagers saw figures moving around the burning building. Nobody was particularly surprised. The rectory was well-known as a haunted house, it was assumed the figures were spectres.

The ghostly reputation of Borley Rectory dates back to the time when it was built. In 1863 the rector, Henry Bull, built the house on what was thought to be the site of a mediaeval convent. As soon as the Bull family took up residence they began seeing strange sights. A shadowy figure, identified as a nun, was seen strolling through the gardens. More dramatically, a phantom coach and horses driven by two headless men was seen galloping across the lawn.

On 2 October 1928, the Bull family was replaced at Borley Rectory by the Reverend Eric Smith and his wife. The new residents were disturbed by the ghost of Henry Bull, and a particularly noisy phantom which created disturbances in the house. Intrigued by the noises, and irritated by his parishioners refusal to visit the house, the Reverend Smith wrote to the *Daily Mirror* asking for the name of a researcher into ghosts. No doubt Smith hoped to rid the house of its ghostly reputation by finding a rational explanation for the phenomena.

The editor of the *Daily Mirror* sent a reporter and then contacted Henry Price, well known for his investigations of haunted houses. Price stayed at Borley for three days and became convinced that the house really was haunted. He believed that a phantom nun and the spirit of Henry Bull wandered through Borley Rectory. Over the following months, Price returned to continue his investigations, but little more was learnt about the reality or not of the hauntings.

Then, on 16 October 1930, a new vicar and his young wife arrived. Lionel Foyster, the new resident, was a relative of the long-dead Henry

A Ghost Hunter's Kit

Supernatural activity is often detected when doors open or noises occur for no natural reason. If you want to discover if a house is haunted you may find the following useful:

Sticky tape placed across doors will break if the door is opened

Tape recorder for recording unusual sounds

Camera for photographing strange phenomena

Thermometer to detect changes in temperature

Notebook and pencil to keep a record of ghostly events

Torch for finding your way in the dark

Sandwiches – even ghost hunters get hungry!

The library at Borley Rectory, used by
Harry Price and his observers.

Bull. Ghostly activity at Borley Rectory at once increased dramatically. Mrs Marianne Foyster saw apparitions, though they remained invisible to others, and the doorbell rang of its own accord several times. Price returned to Borley and found signs of increasing phantom activity.

Most dramatic of this fresh outburst of spectral movements were messages mysteriously found scrawled on the walls of the rectory. These were addressed to Mrs Foyster and demanded help in the form of masses and candles. Their origin remained a mystery.

The shell of Borley
Rectory after the
fire in 1939.

When the Foysters left in 1935, the rectory stood empty for many months. On 19 May 1937, Harry Price moved into the building himself, together with a team of ghost hunters. For a year, Price remained in the house, collecting much evidence of supernatural activity. However, he came to no conclusions and left when his lease expired.

In 1940, Price wrote a book about the strange events at Borley Rectory. It became an instant best-seller and the haunting became famous. Many people were convinced that the events at Borley Rectory provided solid evidence for the existence of ghosts. Others were not so sure.

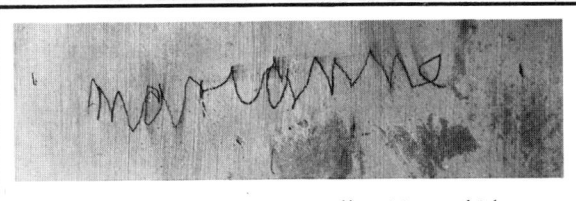

One of the mysterious wall writings which appeared at Borley Rectory.

After Price's death in 1948, odd facts came to light. Several of Price's assistants came forward to say that in many investigations, Price had exaggerated ghostly activities. Some people even suspected Price of faking poltergeist activity and hauntings.

Hoping to find the truth behind the Borley Rectory haunting, the prestigious Society for Psychical Research began an investigation. They examined all of Price's notes and writings. They found that Price had, indeed, distorted facts to make the haunting sound more dramatic and interesting. It was also found that Price had not bothered to investigate some matters properly. Some events Price considered ghostly were found to have normal explanations.

However, despite these criticisms, there remained a small amount of truly ghostly activity at Borley. In 1974 fresh investigations were carried out. Rather than inspect Price's notes, Geoffrey Croom-Hollingsworth journeyed to Borley Rectory itself. He stayed for several weeks and found that visitors to the village were still reporting apparitions.

It was discovered that the phantom nun, long dismissed by critics of Price, had been seen several times. Croom-Hollingsworth actually came face to face with the ghost at a distance of only four metres (12 feet). More impressive still are the tape recordings made by Croom-Hollingsworth and his team. Tapes were set to record inside Borley Church. Although the church was empty, the machines picked up the sounds of footsteps and voices. Perhaps Borley is haunted after all.

The Haunted Church

Just three kilometres (two miles) from Borley lies the town of Sudbury. The church of St Gregory in Sudbury is also said to be haunted, though there is little doubt about the identity of this phantom. It is the ghost of Archbishop Simon Sudbury who died centuries ago.

The Shapeless Horror

Nobody knows what the horror of Number 50 Berkeley Square, London, was, but it claimed the lives of several people during the last century. The terrifying activities centred around an upstairs bedroom in the house, which was otherwise quite normal.

The house was built in the 1730s as part of a fashionable development of large town houses. For more than a century nothing unusual occurred at Number 50, but then the house was left unoccupied for a time. No reason is known why new tenants were difficult to find. Whatever the reason, the house was empty one December night when two sailors by the name of Stephens and Carey wandered into Berkeley Square. The two men had spent all their money and were looking for shelter from the biting cold.

The sailors noticed that Number 50 was empty and broke in. They found an upstairs room which had a convenient drainpipe near the window down which they could escape should anyone search the house. In the early hours of the morning, a passing policeman heard screams coming from Number 50. Running up to the house, the policeman saw a man crash through an upstairs window and fall to the ground. It was Stephens. As he lay dying, Stephens gasped out to the policeman that a horrible half-human creature with claws had attacked him. Later that morning Carey was found. He was raving mad and never recovered.

A few years later the house was leased to a Mr Bentley who moved in with his two daughters. On the day of their arrival, the maid entered an upstairs room and fainted. She spoke of coming across a shapeless horror and made Mr Bentley lock the door permanently.

Soon afterwards Captain Raymond, who was engaged to one of the Bentley girls, heard the story. He decided to spend a night in the room to test his courage. He took with him a pistol and said that if he was in danger he would ring the servant's bell twice.

Soon after midnight the Bentley family heard the bell ring so violently that it was nearly pulled off the wall. Then a pistol shot echoed round the

house. Mr Bentley rushed upstairs and burst into the room. There he found Captain Raymond dead. He had shot himself, though nobody ever found out why.

Towards the end of the last century Lord Lyttleton, a well-known collector of ghost tales, decided to stay in the terrible room. He was determined to take no chances. When he retired to bed, Lord Lyttleton took with him a shotgun loaded with silver coins. During the night, a shapeless creature appeared in the room and sprang at Lyttleton. He raised his gun and fired. The shadowy form collapsed on the ground and vanished. Since then the building has been converted into offices and the horror is no longer seen.

The Faces on the Floor

On 23 August 1971, Dona Maria Gomez Pereira was cooking her family's evening meal in the kitchen of their house in the village of Belmez, southern Spain. Suddenly, Maria heard her grandchild scream. The woman turned round and almost fainted with horror. A unique and disturbing haunting had begun.

On the floor of her kitchen, Dona Maria could see the crudely drawn outline of a face. It had not been there seconds earlier. Dona Maria bent down and tried to clean off the face with a rag and water. As the horrified woman scrubbed away, the eyes of the face opened and stared up at her. Thoroughly frightened, Dona Maria grabbed the child and fled.

When the rest of the Pereira family looked at the picture on the floor, they were truly puzzled. The face gave every appearance of having been painted, but they knew that nobody had had the opportunity to paint it. Miguel Pereira ripped up the floor and laid fresh cement.

Exactly a week later, the face returned. This time it could be made out with startling clarity. The face was that of a man aged about 30 with a small moustache and beard. This time the family did not trouble to dig up the floor. As time passed, the face seemed to change. The face altered to being that of an older man and its mouth opened.

The neighbours in Rodriguez Acosta Street, where the house stood, came to see the face regularly. As the fame of the strange face spread, more and more visitors arrived to view it. Finally, on 2 November, the Mayor of Belmez ordered the face to be dug up and placed behind glass.

Taking advantage of this work, the authorities decided to dig beneath the floor to try to discover a cause for the pictures. At a depth of about three metres (ten feet), they came across a number of human bones. Later research showed that the house had been built on the site of a mediaeval cemetery. The floor was once again replaced with fresh cement.

Turning to the picture itself, the experts began their studies. Though they expected to find paint on the concrete surface, no such substances could be detected. It appeared that the concrete had simply changed colour where the face was formed. No explanation could be found for the phenomenon.

Once removed from its original site, the face began to fade. Meanwhile, a further face appeared on the floor. Beside this third portrait, a fourth formed in early December. Unlike the other three faces, this clearly belonged to a woman. A number of smaller, fainter faces appeared around these two.

In April of the following year, Professor German de Argumosa was present when a new face appeared. It literally grew on the floor while he watched. Starting as a few faint blotches of colour, the face gradually became clearer and more definite. The whole process took several hours to complete. Other faces were reported to appear and vanish within the space of a single day.

After several weeks, voices began to speak. Soft babbling sounds could be heard, as if a large number of people were all talking quietly at once. At irregular intervals loud cries would pierce the general chatter. The voices were always indistinct and nobody could quite catch what was being said.

Theories to account for the strange occurrences were quickly formed. Some people thought that the Pereira family was faking the pictures, or that they were victims of a trick by someone else. Others felt that some terrible deed had been done in the house during the past. It was claimed that the faces were caused by restless spirits. But the most popular theory stated that the faces belonged to those buried in the old cemetery. The spirits, it was said, were unhappy that a house had been built over their graves.

By the end of 1972 no fresh faces were appearing and those which already existed began to fade. The strange voices also ceased to mutter. However, ten years later more faces began to appear. Clearly the unnerving and disturbing haunting was far from over.

The first of the mysterious faces of Belmez appeared quite suddenly and without warning.

Horrors of America

In 1891 the Walsingham family moved into a house in Oakville, Georgia. Before long they were to wish that they had chosen a different home.

As soon as they had taken up residence, the family cleaned the house from top to bottom. Tucked away in a dusty corner, Mr Walsingham found some bones. Thinking that they were animal bones, he threw them out. The ghostly trouble began within a few days.

At first the disturbances were minor and caused little distress. Odd noises were heard at night and floorboards creaked. The Walsinghams believed that the noises were due to the house settling on its foundations. Then a door slammed shut when nobody was near it. Mr Walsingham put the occurrence down to a strong draught. As the days passed, it became increasingly clear that the noises were not being caused by settling foundations or draughts. The bell ropes for summoning servants started ringing of their own accord.

Then the horror started in earnest. Loud shrieks were heard echoing along the corridors and demented laughter rang through the house. Occasionally a loud shout boomed out from beneath the house. Late one evening as the youngest daughter was washing at a basin, the ghost took on a new form. The girl felt somebody touching her on the arm. Thinking her father wanted her attention, the girl turned round. She was horrified to see a disembodied hand clutching her arm. The poor girl shrieked in terror and the hand vanished.

A few days later Mr Walsingham was strolling through the garden when he felt that somebody was following him. He turned round to find no-one. But there was a line of footprints running beside his own in the soft earth.

More unsettling still was the attitude of the ghost to the family's pets. The cat was treated with favour, almost as if it was a friend of the spectre. The dog, however, seemed to hate the spirit. Often the dog would leap to its feet and snarl at someone the Walsinghams could not see. One night, the dog suddenly sprang at its invisible enemy. It leapt forwards and instantly

dropped dead with a broken neck.

By this time the family was growing used to the continual disturbances. They seemed curiously unconcerned by the frightening phenomenon. Their attitude changed dramatically one evening when guests came to dinner. As the family and their friends enjoyed the meal, a drop of red liquid fell from the ceiling on to the table. A second drop followed and it could be seen that the substance was blood. Soon a whole stream of glistening red blood was pouring on to the dinner table. The Walsinghams fled and never returned to the house.

But the story was not yet over. A few weeks after the Walsingham family left the house, a young man named Horace Gunn entered it. He had agreed a large wager that he would remain

The final horror for the Walsingham famiy occured during a dinner party one evening.

in the house overnight. The following morning, Gunn was found lying unconscious on the hall floor with talon-like marks around his throat.

Later, while he recovered in bed, Gunn told his story. He said that everything had gone well until he fell asleep. Gunn had been woken by the sounds of screaming and running footsteps. Then a glowing phantom head had appeared in his room. The head was that of a very old person and had a bloody gash on its forehead.

Leaping out of bed, Gunn ran out of the room. He reached the ground floor, but tripped by the front door. As he struggled to regain his feet, Gunn felt a pair of strong hands closing around his throat. He fought for breath but eventually blacked out and remained unconscious until friends found him next morning.

Another horrific house of evil was revealed to the world in 1979, in the film *The Amityville Horror*. It starred James Brolin as George Lutz, a young man haunted by evil and threatening forces.

The film was based on a book which told the true story of George and Kathleen Lutz. The story opens when the Lutz couple move into an old house in Amityville on Long Island, New York. A short time earlier, in 1974, a horrific series of murders had taken place in the house. One evening 23-year-old Ronald Defoe calmly drugged his entire family and then shot them dead.

Well aware of the house's history, George Lutz called in the local priest to bless his new home. When the priest began his ceremony a disembodied voice ordered him to leave. It seemed that some evil force had taken up residence in the house. That very evening the Lutzs were awoken by odd sounds at the very time that Defoe had carried out his murders.

A few days later, Lutz awoke in the middle of the night to find that the front door had been ripped off its hinges. As the days passed increasingly sinister events occurred. Many of these were reminiscent of poltergeist activity at its worst. Other events were more sinister and diabolic. Within just four weeks, the Lutzs had been thrown into such a state of terror that they fled from the house. They retreated to California and told their story to Jay Anson, who wrote the book.

Various explanations have been advanced for the terrible events which struck the Lutz couple. Some claim that the gruesome murders of Ronald Defoe had been caused by some evil spirit. Defoe himself claimed that "voices" had urged him to commit the murders. Others felt that quite ordinary happenings had been misinterpreted by the Lutzs because they were already nervous about moving into the house. More unkind people suggested that the tale had been deliberately greatly exaggerated and sensationalized.

Whatever the truth about Amityville, an interesting parallel case was reported late last century by a British traveller in the Eastern States of America. It was said that a room in a certain house was inhabited by some strange and terrible force. Anybody who slept in the room for a number of nights became obsessed with the idea of death. At least one unfortunate person came to their senses as they were about to stab members of the family. In order not to embarrass his hosts, the writer did not give the precise location of this awful house. It would be interesting to know just how close it was to the home featured in *The Amityville Horror*.

In the 1890s a chemist's shop in San Francisco was the site of a quite remarkable haunting. It began innocently enough when a man came in with a prescription for some medicine. Edward Marsden, the assistant, took the order. It was a simple one, so he made up the mixture himself. About an hour after the man had left, Marsden was clearing away the bottles of chemicals. To his horror, he found a bottle of deadly poison instead of medicine. Marsden felt he must have added the poison to the prescription. As soon as the patient took his medicine he would die.

By this time, the owner of the shop, James Sweeney, had returned When Marsden told Sweeney what had happened, the older man telephoned the doctor who had written out the prescription. The address of the patient, whose name was Wilson, was obtained and Marsden and Sweeney hurried round. When they arrived, his landlady told them that Wilson had gone to visit relatives and would not be back for a week. Wilson had not left any address and there was no way of contacting him.

Sweeney and Marsden returned home. They realized that all they could do was wait for the dreadful news of Wilson's death Days went by, but no news arrived. Finally the stress must have become too much for Marsden. He died of a heart attack.

But the unhappy spirit of Edward Marsden had not left the chemist's shop. The ghost of the young man was seen several times by the Sweeney family and their maid. Sometimes the ghost was seen strolling along the corridors. But it made its presence felt most often when James Sweeney was mixing up a prescription. Sometimes Sweeney would merely sense that Marsden's spirit was present, but on other occasions the ghost could be seen watching Sweeney closely. Clearly the worried ghost of

The Ghostly Rock Star

The mansion Gracelands in Memphis, Tennessee, was once the home of rock star, Elvis Presley. After his death the house was opened to the public. However, it seems that Presley has not left his old home. Many people have heard his favourite piano play by itself and a few have said that they have seen the ghost of Elvis Presley strolling through the grounds.

Marsden did not want his tragic mistake repeated.

Several days later, a young man strode into Mr Sweeney's shop. It was the Mr Wilson for whom the deadly prescription had been prepared. He told Mr Sweeney that he had taken the medicine, but had suffered no ill effects. Marsden had been mistaken when he thought he had poisoned the mixture.

As Wilson turned to leave he found himself staring into the ghostly face of Edward Marsden. Sweeney saw the apparition at the same moment. The spectre was smiling with relief.

Then, the ghost faded from sight and was never seen again.

It would seem from these tales that ghosts can be as different and varied as humans. The evils which haunted the Lutz and Walsingham families were very different from the benevolent spirit of Edward Marsden.

The film The Amityville Horror *was released in 1978 and starred Rod Steiger, James Brolin and Margot Kidder. The sinister atmosphere of the Lutz house was increased by imaginative lighting and filming.*

TERROR OF THE TOMB

The Return of the Dead

There can be nothing more startling or shocking than meeting a person believed to be dead. Sometimes there is an explanation for these terrifying experiences, but other events defy solution.

In 1629 Joan Norkot was found dead in her house in Hertfordshire. It was assumed that she had committed suicide, so her body was quickly buried. However, neighbours thought that Joan might have been murdered by her husband, Arthur, and her brother-in-law. In an attempt to find out if the wounds were self inflicted or not, the body of Joan Norkot was dug up. The body had been underground for some days and had begun to decompose.

Bracing themselves for an unpleasant inspection, the local vicar and doctor gathered round with the Norkot family. As the inspection was about to begin, the corpse suddenly moved. The witnesses leapt backwards in horror. The dead body opened an eye and pointed at Arthur Norkot. The corpse then lay still once more. The terrified villagers felt that this was proof of guilt and seized the unlucky Arthur Norkot. At a subsequent trial the man was found guilty and hanged.

A very different tale surrounds the reappearance of Margaret Dickson in 1728. She was hanged as a murderer until a doctor pronounced her dead. The body was then taken down and placed in an open coffin for burial. A few hours later, Dickson sat up in her coffin and calmly climbed out. The appearance of the woman caused great fear, until it was realized that she had not been dead when taken from the scaffold.

Perhaps the most curious of all stories of the return of the dead is that of 70-year-old William Harrison, who lived in Gloucestershire in the 17th century. Harrison was responsible for running the estate of Lord Campden. On 16 August 1660, Harrison left his house to collect rents. By the time he had collected the final rent, Harrison was carrying a large amount of money.

Harrison did not return home that evening and the next morning his bloodstained hat was found lying in the road. It was assumed that the elderly man had been attacked by robbers. Suspicion quickly fell on a man called John Perry. Perry was Harrison's assistant. He would have known the amount of money that Harrison was carrying. More suspiciously, Perry could offer no alibi for his movements at the time of the crime.

Perry was arrested and questioned by the local magistrates. He soon broke down and confessed. He said that he and his brother had murdered and robbed Harrison. The body had been thrown into a river and the money hidden at the Perry home by their mother.

Officers of the law searched Perry's home and found some money. Although the river was dragged, Harrison's body was not found. At the subsequent trial, Perry's mother and brother claimed that they were innocent. However, John's confession and other evidence was too strong. The three Perrys were hanged and their bodies chained to gibbets near the scene of the crime.

Two years later, William Harrison returned. He was aghast to hear that the Perrys had been hanged for murdering him. Harrison soon told his story. He had been set upon by a band of robbers and kidnapped. The bandits had then sold Harrison to a Turkish sea captain. He had been taken to the eastern Mediterranean and sold as a slave. It was only after escaping and working a passage on a ship, that Harrison could return home.

Though the mystery of Harrison's disappearance had been solved, nobody could explain the extraordinary behaviour of John Perry. He had confessed and allowed his entire family to be executed for a crime which was never committed.

The bodies of the supposed murderers of William Harrison were hung in iron cages.

The Zombies

Perhaps the most horrific accounts of the living dead come from the West Indies. The cult of voodoo is practised on these islands and many strange stories are told of beings called zombies. It is said that bokors, voodoo magicians, can raise the dead from tombs and force them to work as slaves. It is these walking dead which are the zombies.

Though the idea of zombies seems far fetched, there are numerous cases of zombies actually existing. In 1959 a man was found wandering the streets of a village on Haiti. He glared silently and seemed to be sleepwalking. The man was given a drink of salt water and some food. He then mentioned the name of a woman. When that woman arrived she shrieked in horror. The man was her own nephew who had died and been buried four years earlier.

The American William Seabrook spent several years in Haiti. He took a great interest in voodoo and the story of zombies. An account given by Seabrook tells of a man who offered the services of a gang of workers to a European plantation owner. The workers seemed to act strangely as if in a trance. Unknown to the European the men were zombies. For several weeks the living dead continued to work, until they were fed salty biscuits by mistake. Suddenly the zombies remembered who they were and walked back to their graves. Here they collapsed and died.

From such reports it seems clear that zombies really do exist. However, few people believe that they are really the dead come back to life. It is thought that the bokors have discovered a drug which when taken, gives the impression of death. Having administered the drug, the bokor waits for the victim to be buried and then digs him up. By feeding the hapless victim more drugs, the bokor may be able to keep him senseless and obedient. Such drugged people would be ideal slaves, working without complaint.

Haiti is still an isolated and backward country.

Zombies, the terrible walking dead of Haiti, are said to have glazed eyes and to obey the commands of magicians. Only salt can release a zombie from his terrible state.

Although conditions have improved enormously in recent years, there are still many remote villages where belief in the zombie is widespread. Perhaps bokors are to this day administering drugs and recruiting slave labour.

The Necromancers

Graveyards and tombs have attracted many tales of terror and mystery. None of them is as horrible as the tales of necromancy which occur occasionally through history. This horrible practice of raising the dead in order to obtain information about the future has its origins in the belief that the dead journey to another world. It is thought that through this special experience the dead gain supernatural knowledge not available to the living. It is often said that the newly dead, whose bodies are still intact, still retain links with the living, making them easy to contact and question.

This belief is widespread. Some American Indian tribes would dress the corpse of a chief in ceremonial robes. The dead body was then placed in a circle and asked questions about the future and about hunting possibilities. This practice was most common among the tribes of the north west coast of North America.

According to the Bible, the Witch of Endor raised the spirit of the prophet Samuel in order to answer the questions of King Saul. In the First Book of Samuel, it is stated that the spirit of Samuel appeared when called by a witch. Saul asked why God had turned against him, no doubt hoping to learn how to regain God's favour. Samuel, however, declared that Saul had sinned by not following the instructions of God. He added that Saul and his sons would die on the following day. This information worried Saul for he knew that he must lead his army into battle against the Philistines. The following day, Saul did indeed die in battle, as did his sons. On this occasion at least, the dead spoke the truth.

The ancient Romans also practised necromancy. Roman sorcerers would bury a bell with a corpse. A few days later the body was dug up. In the course of a long ceremony conducted over the body, the bell was rung. It was believed that this would wake the corpse which would then answer any questions put to it.

Perhaps the most famous instance of necromancy occurred in the 16th century in the churchyard of Walton-le-Dale, Lancashire. The event was recorded by John Dee, a well-known and highly respected mathematician, who had an unfortunate interest in the occult. This interest nearly caused his death.

As a young man, Dee studied both at the University of Cambridge and in Europe. Dee wrote a large number of complicated and successful mathematical books. One of these was a study of the calendar and suggestions for its improvement, while another work suggested many advancements to the science of navigation.

These successful works led to Dee being made a professor at Cambridge University. In the early 1550s, at the age of 24, Dee became fascinated by astrology. He cast the horoscopes of many noble men and women. This came to the notice of the authorities and Dee was promptly arrested. He was charged with being a heretic and trying to murder Queen Mary through black magic. Dee spent two years in jail and was lucky to escape with his life. However, this bad experience did not deter him.

Leaving astrology, Dee began to study alchemy and conducted many experiments. John Dee then met an Irishman by the name of Edward Kelly who claimed to be an expert practitioner of black magic. Among many other claims, Kelly stated that he had taken part in a necromantic episode at Walton-le-Dale in Lancashire. He stated that, together with a man named Paul Waring, he drew a magic circle on the ground and conducted a ceremony to raise the dead. Kelly said a corpse then came to life and he asked it several questions. However, it later proved that Kelly was a cheat and liar. Though Dee never had any doubts about this attempt at necromancy, others have. They suggest that Kelly faked the whole incident in order to gain the favour of the rich Dee.

Later experiments into the horrible art of necromancy by various practitioners has suggested that beings from the spirit world may be called upon. However, the words of Eliphas Levi who tried such an experiment in 1854 and summoned up a demon are a warning to be taken seriously. He stated that "I regard the practice as destructive and dangerous."

A famous example of necromancy occurred in the 16th century in the churchyard of St Leonard's, a church in Walton-le-Dale, Lancashire.

The Bodysnatchers

Perhaps the most horrible crime in history is that perfected by the Edinburgh crooks William Burke and William Hare. Strangely enough neither of these men was actually Scottish. Burke was an Irishman and Hare came from England.

During the 1820s, when Burke and Hare practised their gruesome trade, the number of human corpses available for dissection was severely restricted. Medical students were, therefore, willing to pay high prices for bodies which had been cleared by the authorities. A few such students were unscrupulous enough to pay for corpses whatever their origin.

This demand was satisfied by men willing to rob the freshly dug graves of their occupants. Burke and Hare began robbing graves in the middle 1820s. They sold the corpses they stole to the 30-year-old Doctor Robert Knox. Knox was at this time the conservator of the Edinburgh Museum of Comparative Anatomy.

His lectures, accompanied by the dissection of corpses provided by Burke and Hare, proved to be exceptionally popular. Knox soon gained the prestigious position of head of the Anatomical School of Edinburgh. His demand for corpses quickly outstripped the number that Burke and Hare could steal from churchyards.

The two men, therefore, turned to producing their own supply of corpses. Selecting one of Edinburgh's destitute population, Burke and Hare would ply their victim with drink and persuade him to enter Hare's home. Once the victim was thoroughly drunk, Burke and Hare would suffocate him. The fresh corpse would then be sold to Knox.

After 15 people had fallen victim to the murderous activities of Burke and Hare, suspicion was aroused. The two men were arrested. Hare gave evidence against Burke to save his own neck and his testimony convicted Burke, who was hanged. Hare died in poverty some 30 years later. Although it was not proved that Knox had been involved in the murders, many people thought he knew the terrible origin of the corpses he bought. Knox lost his job and never recovered his reputation.

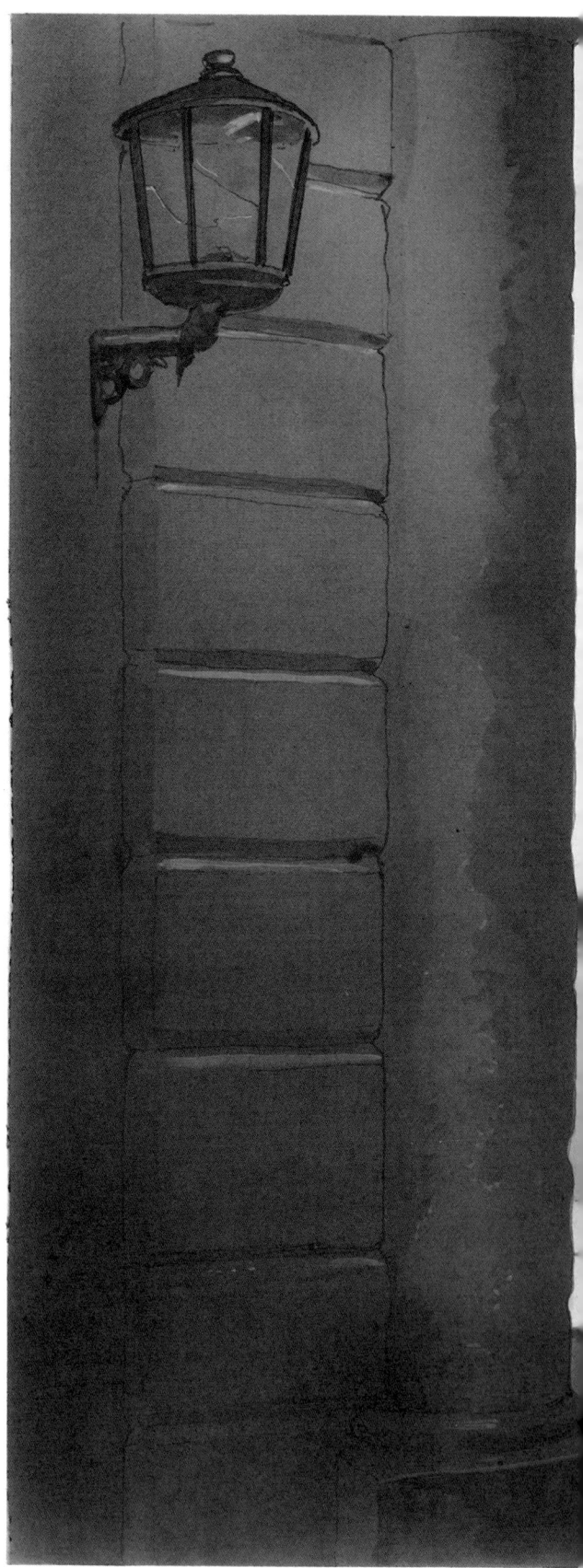

Horrific Burials

The pagan societies which existed centuries ago often demanded complicated burials, some of which would appear frightful today. One of the earliest beliefs was that the dead should be buried with any objects which would be useful in the afterlife. Since this otherworld was imagined to be very similar to earthly life, everyday objects were buried in graves. A farmer might be buried with a plough and a warrior with a sword.

Important people were buried with more impressive objects. The early graves of Chinese and Egyptian kings contained the bodies of servants and slaves. At first these unfortunate people were slaughtered during the funeral of the monarch. Later, statues of slaves were buried with the dead king. These represented the servants who were expected to accompany their master to the world of the dead.

Later societies dispensed with such representations of humans. The 7th century Anglo-Saxon burial at Sutton Hoo in England contained richly-ornamented jewellery and

The horrific guardians of a Schythian tomb.

valuable goods. All these were placed within a ship which had probably belonged to the early English king who was buried within it, but no human servants were buried.

Perhaps the most horrible tombs of all were those constructed for the kings of the Scythians. These ferocious and warlike people inhabited the grassy plains of southern Russia in about 500 BC and continually raided the territory of neighbouring peoples. Their warriors were archers who rode fine horses and could attack or retreat at lightning speed.

To protect the tombs of the dead kings, specially privileged warriors would be sacrificed. The bodies were then tied to wooden frames and mounted on dead horses, likewise attached to frames. Surrounded by the slaughtered bodies of his fiercest warriors, the king of the Scyths rested in peace. As years passed the flesh of the horrific guardians of the tomb rotted away. Eventually the dead king would be surrounded by a gruesome guard of skeletons.

The Unquiet Dead

In the churchyard of Oistin's Bay on the island of Barbados in the West Indies stands a burial vault. It contains no bodies because of a terrifying series of events which took place there early in the 19th century.

The vault is near to the entrance of Christ Church graveyard and was excavated out of the ground so that its roof is at ground level. The floor, walls and roof of the vault are constructed of large blocks of solid limestone. The only way in or out of the tomb is by way of the sunken doorway built on one side.

The tomb was intended as a family vault for the Goddard family. On 31 July 1807 the body of Mrs Thomasina Goddard was buried in the tomb. The entrance was then blocked with a large stone door. The edges of the door were sealed with cement. The year following the burial of Mrs Goddard, the vault was sold to the wealthy Chase family. The Chases owned large estates on the island, and they also owned many black slaves who worked on the land.

On 22 February 1808, the vault was opened and the tiny coffin of young Mary Anna Maria Chase was placed inside. The vault was then sealed again. Four years later, on 6 July 1812, another child of the Chase family, named Dorcas, died. Once more the tomb was opened and the coffin placed inside.

Only a month later Mr Thomas Chase, the father of the two children, died. When the vault was opened this time a scene of chaos was seen by the mourners. The two coffins of Mary and Dorcas Chase had been set on end at the far side of the vault and that of Mrs Goddard had been moved slightly to one side.

Nobody could imagine what had caused the disarray. The vault showed no signs of having been broken into, yet the three coffins had very definitely moved. To make the affair more mysterious, the two Chase coffins were made of lead and were extremely heavy. Yet these two were moved further than Mrs Goddard's wooden coffin. The coffins were laid back on the floor and that of Thomas Chase placed beside them.

Four years later, on 25 September 1816, the

vault was opened to take the coffin of a relative of the Chase family named Samuel Ames. Again the coffins within the tomb had been interfered with. All four coffins were scattered around the vault. It was as if some giant had flung the heavy lead coffins around the small room. It was noticed, however, that Mrs Goddard's coffin had not been moved. After replacing the coffins, the tomb was sealed.

By this time the members of the Chase family were becoming concerned. They thought that somebody with a grudge against them might be seeking some macabre revenge. At first it was thought that the black slaves might be responsible. However they denied the charge and showed such fear of the restless coffins that they were discounted as culprits.

When, on 17 July 1819, another burial was due to take place at the vault, the official authorities began to take an interest in the sinister happenings. Lord Combermere, the governor of the island, attended the funeral. The coffins, as expected, were found scattered throughout the vault. This time, after the coffins were replaced, Lord Combermere scattered sand across the floor. He then added his personal seal to the concrete fixing the door in place.

Several months later, Lord Combermere ordered the tomb to be opened. He carefully inspected his seals. The door had not been disturbed. When the vault was opened, the coffins, except that of Mrs Goddard, were once again scattered around the room. The sand on the floor showed no signs of footprints. Clearly nobody had entered the vault. Thoroughly terrified, the Chase family moved their dead to other graves and the sinister vault lay empty.

Several suggestions have been put forward to solve the strange mystery of the Chase vault. Some point out that the coffin of Mrs Goddard remained undisturbed and that it was the only wooden coffin. Perhaps some strange force was acting like a magnet on the lead coffins, pulling them out of position. Other people suggest that the spirit of Mrs Goddard resented members of another family being buried with her. Perhaps her ghost was responsible for the movements. The truth is, however, that nobody knows what made the coffins and their dead bodies move.

Cheating the Tomb

There is an old belief that the moment of a person's death is decided by some great power. The activities of some ghosts seem to indicate that on rare occasions, some people are protected from what seems to be certain death. They somehow manage to cheat the grave.

Perhaps the most famous such incident occurred in 1890 at a large Irish mansion near Tullamore. A guest at the house was Lord Dufferin, a distinguished British diplomat. In the middle of the night, Lord Dufferin was woken by strange noises coming from the garden. He got out of bed and looked through the window.

In the moonlight, Dufferin could see a man carrying a large box. As the man came nearer, Dufferin realized that the box was a coffin. When Dufferin cried out in horror, the man turned to look at him. The stranger's face was twisted into an expression of hatred. Then the man simply vanished.

A year later Lord Dufferin was in a Paris hotel attending a conference. Wishing to visit the 5th floor, Lord Dufferin called the lift. But when it arrived, Lord Dufferin stepped back in horror. The lift attendant had the same face as the ghost he had seen in Ireland. Dufferin refused to enter the lift. While he tried to recover from the shock, the lift set off for the 5th floor. Suddenly the cable snapped and the lift fell down its shaft, killing all the occupants.

Claude Sawyer also owed his life to a nocturnal vision. While sailing on the ship *Waratah* in 1909, Sawyer dreamt he saw a figure waving a sword and bloodstained rag in his face. After experiencing the vision three times, Sawyer left the ship. Days later, the *Waratah* sank with all its crew.

More active was the phantom which saved an American car factory worker in 1964. The man felt himself pulled backwards by a ghostly apparition. Seconds later the machine on which he had been working ran out of control. If it had not been for his phantom guardian the man would have been killed.

During the Second World War, a British soldier in Burma was shaken awake one night by a soldier he did not recognize. The stranger told the man that his senior officer wanted to see him. Scrambling to his feet, the soldier hurried to the officer, only to find him fast asleep. At that moment Japanese artillery opened fire. One of the first shells landed at the precise spot where the soldier had been sleeping.

Less lucky were the guests at an aristocratic dinner party in France late in the 18th century. One of the guests, the Marquis de Cazotte, suddenly knew exactly how all the other guests

would die and passed the gruesome tidings on to his companions. As the years passed, despite the forewarnings, the predictions of the marquis all came true. Sometimes there can be escape from the grave and sometimes there cannot.

THE BLOODSUCKERS

The Vampires of Transylvania

The vampire has become a familiar character in horror stories and films. In 1922 a silent motion picture called *Nosferatu* launched the nocturnal bloodsucker on to the big screen. Dozens of other films have followed. The attitude of most people to these tales of the undead is that they are entertaining stories and nothing more. However, in Eastern Europe, vampires are believed to exist. Historical documents record instances of vampires terrorizing small communities.

The traditional vampire is a gruesome being. It takes the form of a dead person who has not truly died but can only be killed by a wooden stake through the heart. The body and tortured soul of the supposedly dead rises from the grave at night to prey on the blood of living victims. It is said that the vampire needs to drink blood in order to satisfy a craving and hunger which torments it. Vampires appear as thin, pasty-faced individuals with pointed ears and long teeth who cannot stand daylight. Their piercing eyes are said to be particularly distinctive. This terrifying creature casts no reflection in a mirror. Each day, it is said that the vampire returns to its grave to rest until night falls again when it will set off in search of fresh victims.

This picture of a living corpse sounds quite ridiculous, but there are numerous reports of real vampires. These accounts are especially common from the years between 1500 and 1800. There seemed to be an epidemic of vampires in those years across Eastern Europe. One of the central areas of vampire activity was Transylvania, a remote region of modern Romania.

Many of the tales originated from uneducated

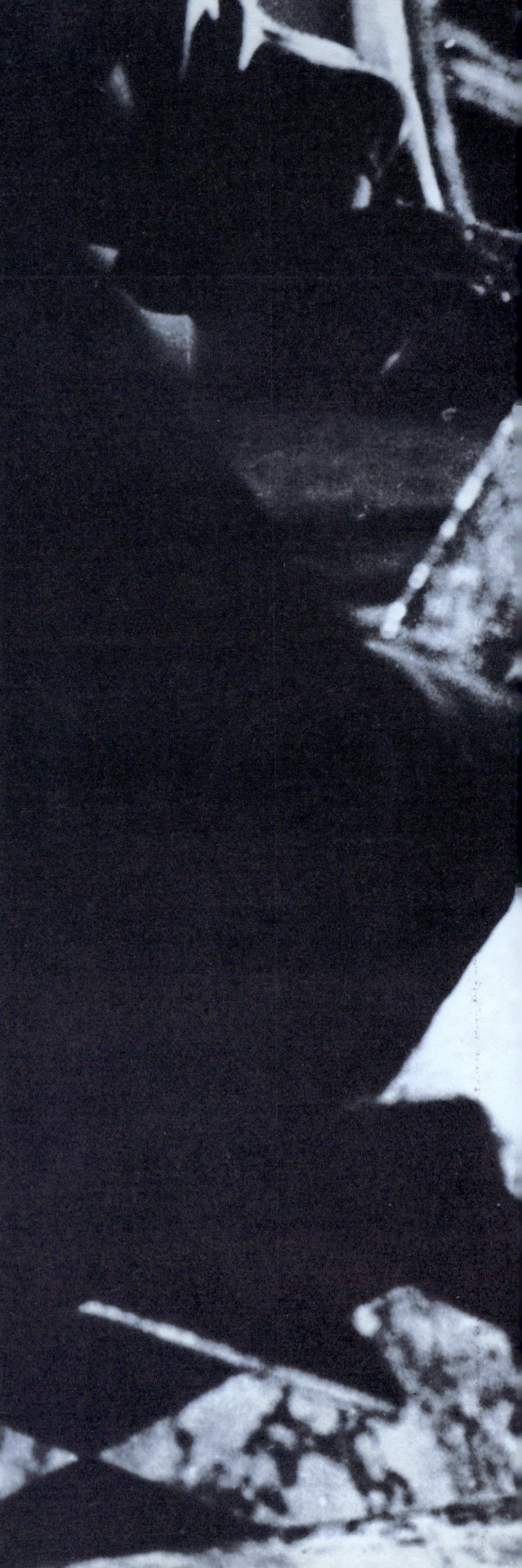

Christopher Lee plays Count Dracula in a 1958 movie made by Hammer Films. Vampires are said to be repelled by the crucifix (inset).

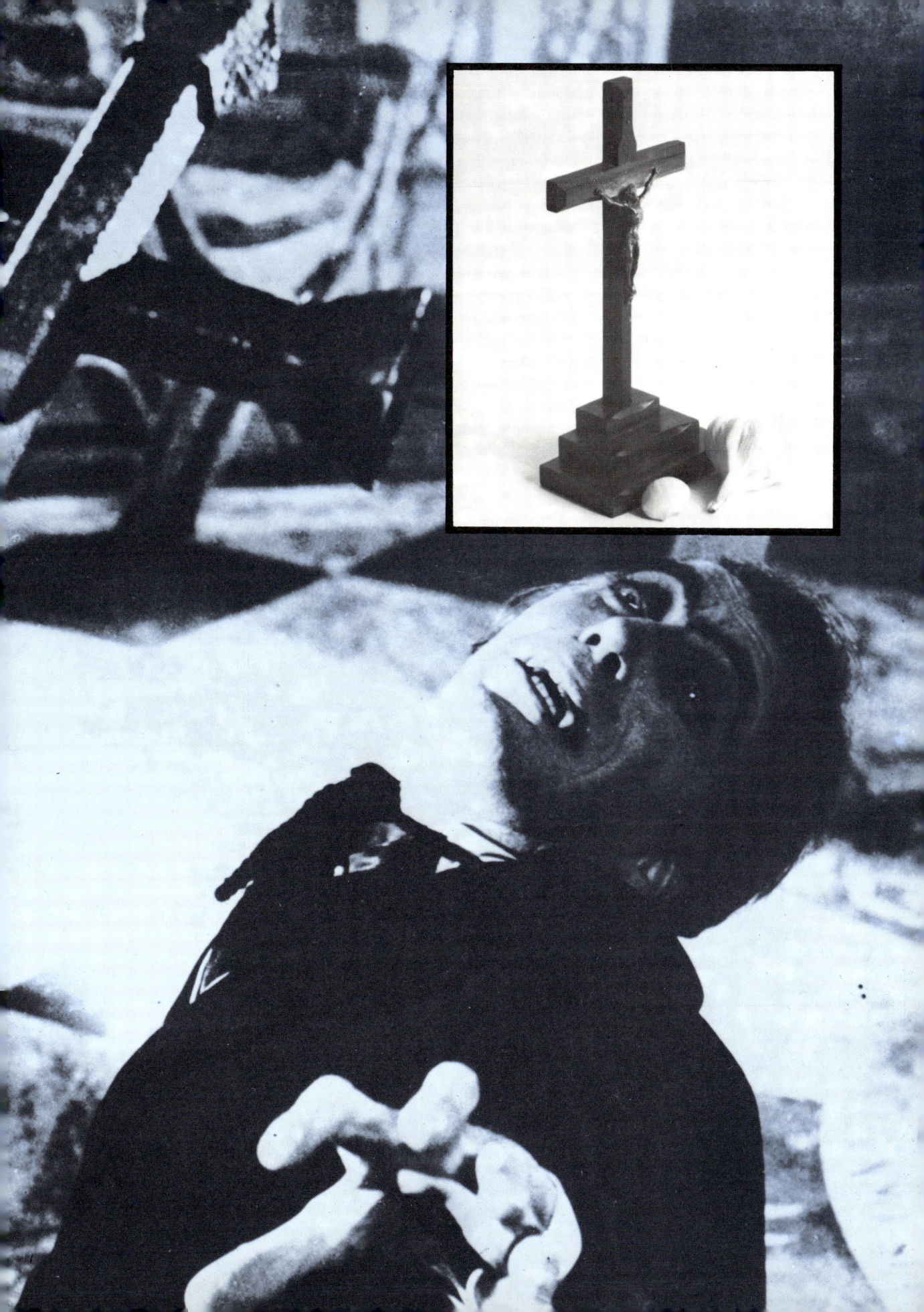

peasants who were famous for their super-stitions. Sceptics might say that such people cannot be trusted to be objective when dealing with a subject as sensational as vampirism.

However, several reports were written down by educated gentlemen, doctors and clergymen. Perhaps the most famous of these cases occurred in 1732. A farming family in what is now part of Yugoslavia claimed that they were being plagued by a vampire. For some reason this particular case came to the attention of the government. Determined to discover the truth, the authorities sent out a group of investigators. Clearly nobody wished to take chances, so the deputation was accompanied by 24 soldiers and an officer.

When the investigation committee arrived at the village, they found the entire population to be nervous and jumpy. The family in question had lost four members to the vampire in only a month. The previous evening a young girl had been attacked and lay ill in her bed. The corpse suspected as being the vampire was that of a man who had died three years earlier.

The investigators at once visited the church-yard, while the frightened villagers kept at a distance. When they opened the dead man's grave they did not find the skeleton they expected. Instead the corpse gave every appear-ance of simply being asleep. Distinctly worried, the soldiers drove a stake through the heart of the corpse and hacked off its head. The grave was resealed and the village was not troubled by the vampire again.

Stories such as this support the view that vampires do actually exist. However, another explanation has been put forward. In past centuries medical science was fairly primitive. It is possible that people in comas or trances might have been thought to be dead. If this were the case, a living person might be buried. If the grave of such a person were to be opened a few days later, the "corpse" would be found to be still warm and breathing. This might account for the origin of many vampire stories.

Traditionally, vampires live in cemeteries and crawl out of their tombs at night in search of victims. This is Highgate Cemetery, London.

Vampires Around the World

Tales of vampires are usually found in Eastern Europe, but the occasional story brings the blood-sucking menace closer to home. Perhaps the best known of these concerns the house Croglin Grange in Cumbria.

One autumn early in the last century, Croglin Grange was rented by a family consisting of two adult brothers and a sister. For months the three were happy. But everything changed on a hot evening the following summer. The girl went to bed, but could not sleep because of the heat. In the dead of night, a hideous, brown figure broke into the girl's room and bit her savagely on the neck. As the young woman screamed, the creature, which resembled a shrivelled man, leapt out of the window and fled before the brothers could arrive.

In order to help the sister recover from the shock, the family moved to Switzerland for several weeks and then returned to Croglin Grange. Thinking that some dangerous lunatic might be responsible for the attack, the brothers kept loaded pistols ready in case the intruder returned.

After several weeks, the girl awoke in the middle of the night to see the ugly face of the creature peering in through her window. Struck with utter terror the girl screamed as loud as she could. The figure at once fled. The brothers ran to the girl's rescue and fired their pistols, hitting the hideous thing in the leg. They then chased after the fleeing creature. The limping figure ran into a churchyard and dived into an old family crypt.

(Left) the vampire of Croglin Grange and (above) a man was attacked by a woman in New York.

The next day, the men returned to the crypt and broke into it. There they found a coffin containing the creature they had chased the night before, sleeping peacefully. Hauling the body outside, the men burnt it to ashes.

The story of the vampire of Croglin Grange is told in the memoirs of Augustus Hare who claims he was told the story by the owners of the building. Though it is a chilling story which brings the horror of the vampire close to home, it is very probably entirely fictional. There is no such place as Croglin Grange, nor was there in the last century. The churchyard described in the story does not contain a family vault at all. Unfortunately for those who like to believe in such tales, it would seem that there never was a vampire in Cumbria.

Though the vampire may not exist, there can be little doubt that some people feel a lust for blood. For example, the 15th century French nobleman, Gilles de Rais, delighted in draining blood from his victims and then drinking it.

In 1924 Fritz Haarman followed a similarly bloody career in Hanover. It is thought that he committed 50 murders to satisfy his craving before he was caught. The punishment was suitably traditional for a vampire. He was beheaded with an ancient, two-handed sword.

More recently, a young man in New York received a severe shock when he took a young woman out for the evening. As they were saying goodnight, the girl suddenly pounced on him and bit his neck until blood spurted out. The woman was later unable to explain her actions. She seemed to have been suddenly overwhelmed by a strong desire to bite the man.

During the 1970s mysterious figures were seen in London's Highgate Cemetery and several people claimed that they saw a huge vampire hovering over the graves. This resulted in "vampire hunts" in the burial ground. However, some of the hunters broke open tombs and were arrested for desecration.

The Greatest Vampire of All

Dracula, the most famous vampire of all, never existed, although many people believe he did. The real person who has become identified with the vampire legend was a successful medieval warlord of the 15th century.

Vlad Dracula, whose name means nothing more sinister than Vlad, son of Dracul, became Prince of Wallachia in 1456. He at once set about enlarging and strengthening his principality. Years of warfare with Turkey followed, during which Dracula frequently resorted to terrorist activities. He succeeded in driving the Turks back into the Balkans after a particularly bloody campaign.

However, Dracula's success was to be short lived. He was robbed of his principality by a rival Christian warlord and restricted to court. Some years later, Dracula obtained a minor position in a Christian army launching a fresh crusade against his old enemies, the Turks. The real Dracula died a hero's death when he was killed in 1476 fighting the Turks. To the Romanians, Vlad Dracula remains a powerful national hero.

However, Dracula's liking for torture and murder became well known, especially his habit of impaling the bodies of his enemies on tall spikes. This particularly nasty habit reached a gruesome climax when he impaled the bodies of 20,000 defeated Turks. The hideous forest was erected in the path of a second invading Turkish army. When the invaders came across the terrible sight, they turned and fled home rather than face the ruthless count.

This bloodthirsty reputation came to the notice of an Irish writer, Bram Stoker, in the 19th century. At the time, Stoker was looking for the subject for a horror novel. Stories of vampires and of Dracula were told to him by a Hungarian friend. He found the name of the long-dead Wallachian prince evocative and the subject of vampires suitably spine-chilling.

Weaving the two together, Bram Stoker created a novel of startling originality and gruesome horror. The story opens with a young English estate agent, named Jonathan Harker, travelling to see a Transylvanian nobleman interested in buying a house in England. The Transylvanian villagers whom he meets seem terrified of Count Dracula, but do not explain why.

When Harker arrives at Dracula's castle he is impressed by the richness of the decoration. However as the days pass, Harker becomes increasingly uneasy. He sees the count only after dark and there are no mirrors in the castle. Gradually, Harker realizes that Dracula is a vampire and he flees from Transylvania. However, Dracula follows the young Englishman to Whitby Abbey and the novel narrates their supernatural struggle for survival to a terrifying climax.

Though the novel *Dracula* is very long and to modern readers may seem dull in several places, it remains a classic example of horror literature. The character of Dracula is so compelling that it quickly became the image of a vampire for many people. Dracula is tall and aristocratic. Handsome and elegant, Dracula is able to mix with the finest society with ease. The dramatic contrast between this attractive, if slightly sinister, man and his activities as a vampire are part of the fascination of the portrayal.

The tale of Dracula was made into a stage play in 1925. Then in 1931 the actor Bela Lugosi took the role of the count in a classic horror film which has rarely been bettered. Over the following years, the character returned to the screen many times. Sometimes the original Bram Stoker story was used, but more often Dracula appeared in a quite different story. The vampire count has probably died on screen more times than any other creature.

The films with which most modern audiences are familiar are the movies made by the British company Hammer Films. They began with *Dracula*, a film of the original story, in 1958. This was so successful that a whole series of vampire films, with titles such as *The Brides of Dracula* and *Dracula Has Risen From the Grave*, followed. Frequent television repeats of the films and reprints of the original book seem to ensure that Dracula will continue to symbolize the vampire to many people.

Count Dracula rests in his coffin.

THE WITCHES

The Nature of Witchcraft

There can be no doubt that witches exist. Or more accurately people who believe that they are witches exist. Many different views of witchcraft have been expressed and various theories advanced. Although many of these ideas are firmly believed by those who voice them, some theories contradict each other. It is difficult to know just exactly what a witch is supposed to be.

According to ancient folklore and beliefs held in past centuries, the witch had a very definite form. The witch was almost always a woman, often one who lived alone. She could, however, be either young or old and often lived close to other witches. She was not always the solitary old hag of modern popular imagination.

These witches were thought to be able to call upon supernatural powers to perform certain deeds. Often witches were skilled in mixing magic potions. A woman who was able to extract medicinal properties from various plants might have been thought to be a witch. Sometimes the witch might use such powers to perform good deeds, on other occasions a witch might use her powers for evil. On the other hand, a witch might be neither exclusively good nor evil. She might work entirely for her own benefit.

A common belief was that witches could change themselves into hares. In this shape they would visit the cattle of local farmers and steal milk. Stories concerning this belief usually end when a farmer attacks the hare, perhaps cutting off a paw. It is later found that a woman in the village has mysteriously lost a hand. In this way the witch is identified and her power broken. These tales show that people really did believe that witches existed, and that their powers were very real.

Towards the end of the Middle Ages, the belief grew that witches indulged in devil worship. This evil and dangerous practice was vigorously repressed by the Christian church. Anybody suspected of being a witch might be

(Below) James VI of Scotland (James I of England) interrogating suspected witches.
(Right) the popular image of a witch.

The 16th century witches of North Berwick were said to have danced around the church and plotted to kill King James VI.

arrested and tried as a criminal. The punishment for witchcraft was death. Many people were executed as witches during the 16th and 17th centuries. In Europe, alleged witches were usually burnt at the stake but in Britain they were hanged.

The beliefs of country folk and the Church regarding witchcraft are the only views which have been handed down from the past. They were written by people who were not witches and only reported what they saw. Some of these people did not believe that witches existed at all. They thought that the tales of spells and potions were based on superstition, and that the unfortunate women executed for witchcraft were innocent victims. Other writers not only believed in witchcraft, but felt that there was a worldwide conspiracy of witches determined to overthrow Christianity.

In more recent years, witches have started to speak out for themselves. They claim that witchcraft is a respectable religion, which is separate from but not hostile to Christianity.

Witches claim that their beliefs form the pagan religion which existed in Europe before Christianity arrived. During their ceremonies they call upon old gods and goddesses. Most modern witches claim that they practise good or white magic, however it seems likely that a few witches are involved in evil practices.

There is, however, no way of verifying these claims made by modern witches. The true nature of witchcraft remains obscure.

Nuns and Witches

Outbreaks of apparent witchcraft and devilry in convents have attracted particular notoriety because of the Holy establishment in which they take place. The first such event to become famous occurred in 1491 in a convent in northern France. A group of nuns suddenly fell into fits. They barked like dogs and slobbered and ran on all fours like animals. The fits ceased when one of the nuns left the convent. It was assumed at the time that she was a witch and had cast spells on the other nuns. However, it now seems likely that the nuns had suffered from an outbreak of mass hysteria.

The Salem Witch Hunt

Perhaps the most famous trial of witches took place in the American village of Salem in the 1690s. This particular case is fascinating for it began with a group of worried villagers faced with a real problem and resulted in the execution of several innocent women. It has been held up as a prime example of the terrible effects of suspicion and bigotry.

The savagery with which the witch hunt was pursued seems all the more dramatic because of the sober and respectable background against which it raged. The village of Salem, in Essex County, Massachusetts, was in 1691 a fairly typical Puritan village of North America: the ordinary villagers were God-fearing and educated. Although witchcraft was believed to exist, it was not thought of as a problem likely to affect Salem. A few horrific stories of witchcraft came across the Atlantic but there was no indication of the horror to come.

The event which made Salem so famous began early in 1692. Seven girls, aged between nine and 20, organized and took part in a seance. Their aim was to try to foretell the future. Instead a gruesome spectral coffin materialized and then vanished. A few days later, the girls suddenly collapsed in fits. They complained that

The Witch House at Salem, where the preliminary hearings of the trial were held.

they were being attacked by invisible beings. Several of the blows and scratches felt by the girls actually left physical marks on their bodies. It did, indeed, seem that some force was tormenting them.

Two of the girls were promptly taken to another village by their parents and quickly recovered. The remaining five girls stayed in Salem and continued to suffer attacks.

After several weeks of such inexplicable attacks, the girls announced the source of the violence. They said that they were bewitched by three local women. The accused were a slave named Tituba, and two elderly women, Sarah Osburn and Sarah Good. On 29 February, the three women were arrested and brought before magistrates.

At first the judges, John Corwin and John Hathorne, seemed unsure what to do. Cotton Mather, a respected local churchman was asked for his advice. He suggested caution in accepting the girls' evidence. Mather argued that if the

(Below) the Salem girls denouncing one of the locals, George Jacobus, in court. (Right) the title page of a contemporary book concerning the Salem trials.

The Wonders of the Invisible World:

Being an Account of the

TRYALS

OF

Several Witches,

Lately Excuted in

NEW-ENGLAND:

And of several remarkable Curiosities therein Occurring.

Together with,

I. Obfervations upon the Nature, the Number, and the Operations of the Devils.

II. A fhort Narrative of a late outrage committed by a knot of Witches in Swede-Land, very much refembling, and fo far explaining, that under which New-England has laboured.

III. Some Councels directing a due Improvement of the Terrible things lately done by the unufual and amazing Range of Evil-Spirits in New-England.

IV. A brief Difcourfe upon thofe Temptations which are the more ordinary Devices of Satan.

By COTTON MATHER.

The English settlers of North America took their witchcraft beliefs with them and would tell their children the stories of English witches such as Elizabeth Sawyer, executed in 1621.

Devil could attack young girls he could also make them accuse innocent people.

Meanwhile the judges had brought Sarah Good into court. As soon as she entered, the girls collapsed in fits and appeared to suffer blows. When they recovered they claimed that Sarah Good's spirit had attacked them. Little more evidence was needed and the three accused women were thrown into jail. It did not seem to occur to anybody that Sarah Good was unlikely to attack the girls in front of witnesses.

A few days later, the bewitched girls suffered more attacks. This time, they claimed, the guilty person was Martha Corey, a respectable churchgoer. This accusation was followed by that of another woman, Rebecca Nurse. Though Corwin and Hathorne seemed surprised and concerned that two apparently good

women should be accused, they did not hesitate. The women were arrested.

By this time, the evidence of the girls was being accepted without question. At the same time the girls' evidence began to take on signs of hysteria. Anybody who expressed doubt about the girls' sincerity soon found themselves accused. One of the first such victims was John Proctor, who employed one of the bewitched girls.

He appeared in the court one day and hauled his servant home, declaring the whole affair to be nonsense. Once back at her duties, the girl recovered from her fits. Within days Proctor, his wife and the servant girl had all been accused of witchcraft and arrested. The number of people being named as witches grew alarmingly. At the same time, the fear of the inhabitants of Salem increased enormously. It seemed that a terrible evil was being uncovered in the village. Soon it was thought that any means of destroying the wicked cult of witchcraft were justified. On 10 June an accused woman named Bridget Bishop was hanged.

The atmosphere of fear and suspicion lasted all summer. By the end of October a total of 20 people had been executed on charges of witchcraft by the court. A further 200 people had been arrested. The finger of suspicion had even been pointed at the wife of the Governor of Massachusetts.

Suddenly the excesses became too much. Any single person speaking against the trials was liable to be accused in turn. However, on 29 October the clergy of the state approached the General Court and asked for the court to be disbanded. The accusations and executions ceased at once.

Within a few months, most of those under arrest were released without charges being brought. Even those who had been executed were pardoned posthumously and their property returned to their heirs. However, the young girls who had acted as accusers continued to suffer occasional attacks and never completely regained their sanity.

In the light of modern research it seems clear that the girls were suffering from a form of hysteria. This can, in extreme cases, cause actual

physical effects similar to those experienced by the Salem girls. The fear which they whipped up in the community is not so easy to explain. However, it seems to have struck at a time when witchcraft was firmly believed to be evil. The sudden revelation that witches were active locally may have been enough to strike terror into the hearts of god-fearing folk. The Salem witch trials remain as a salutary warning of how fear and superstition can affect a perfectly normal community.

Cotton Mather who was involved with the Salem trials. (Below) demons and angels struggle for the soul of a dying man.

The Deadly Toll of Witch Hunts

During late 1631 and early 1632, the town of Oppenau in central Germany was gripped by a frenzy of witch hunting. The terrified citizens believed that a whole colony of witches existed in the town and was working evil. In the space of just nine months, one in every 12 inhabitants of the town were executed for witchcraft.

Witches and the Devil

The belief which caused the great persecutions of witches during the 16th and 17th centuries was that they were the servants of the Devil. This belief seems to have formed towards the end of the Middle Ages. In 1484 Pope Innocent VIII declared that witchcraft was a wicked heresy. Whether witches were using their powers for good or evil was not important. The source of their supposed powers was the Devil, so all their actions were thought to be evil.

The connection with the Devil was revealed through both theological argument and the confessions of witches. From these pieces of testimony a remarkable picture of organized devil-worship can be built up. From the evidence gathered, the cult would seem to have been widespread across Europe and to have formed a powerful force opposed to Christianity.

Covens, or groups of 13 witches, would meet

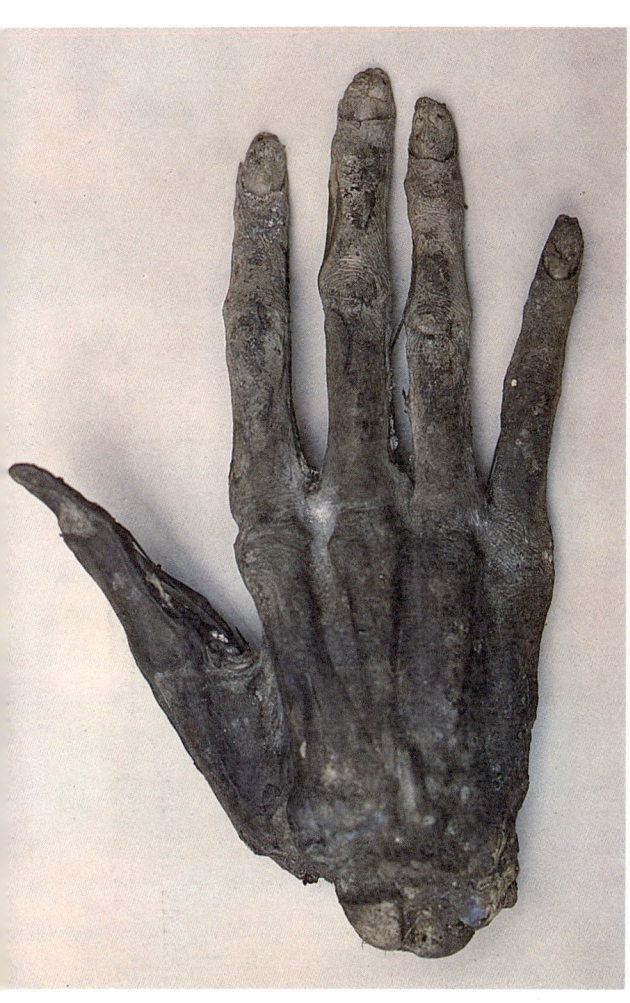

many supposed devil's marks were simply birthmarks.

Very often a witch would make a pact with the Devil. Most of these seem to have been verbal agreements by which the witch gave his or her soul to the Devil in return for wealth or some other gift. However, some pacts were made in writing and one remarkable document has survived from the 17th century.

It was written by Father Grandier, a French priest, at Loudun in 1633. In the document the man promises to "do as much evil as I can and lead as many other people into evil as shall be possible". Grandier signed the document in blood. Around the signature of Grandier are many strange marks and signs. It is claimed that these patterns are the signatures of demons accepting the pact with Grandier.

The practices of witches were seen by the Church as diabolical versions of baptism, confession and the body of the 12 disciples. These instances of devil-worship were bad enough, but the international nature of the cult truly frightened the investigators.

The strange signatures on this document are claimed to be those of demons.

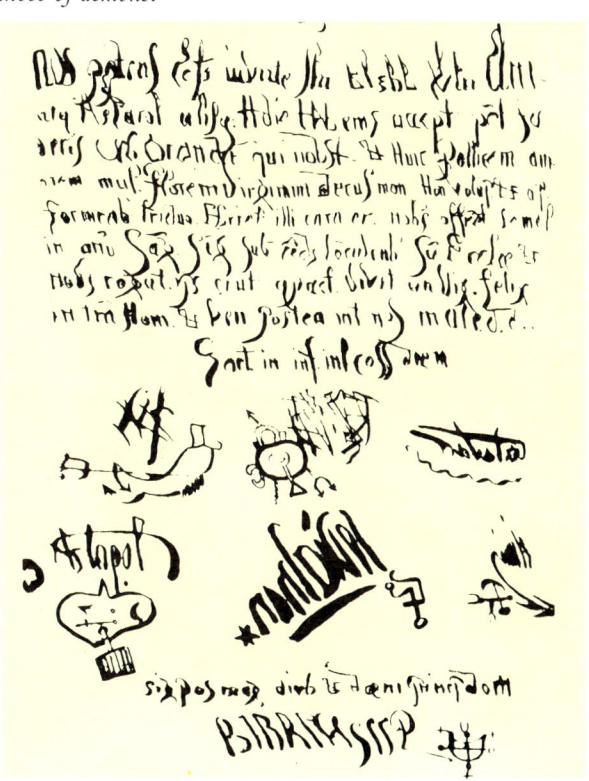

(Left) a supposed portrait of the demon Cassiel. (Above) a hand of glory. Cut from a hanged man, pickled and used as a candle holder, the hand was supposed to open locked doors and prevent people from waking.

regularly to conduct ceremonies and feast together. According to several confessions, the leader of a coven was known as the devil. At each meeting, or esbat, the witches had to tell their devil how many wicked deeds they had performed since the previous meeting.

New members of the coven might be initiated into the cult at an esbat. They would be asked solemnly to accept the practices of witchcraft at the expense of Christianity. This may have involved ritually stamping on a cross. A renaming ceremony would follow, after which the newcomer would receive the "devil's mark". This skin blemish was said to be caused by the Devil touching the initiate. However,

The punishments handed out to witches varied between countries and often within a country itself. Some witches were merely fined or imprisoned, but some were put to death. On the continent, execution usually took the form of burning alive. In England, however, this agonisingly slow death was abandoned in favour of hanging. The 17th century illustration (above) shows a group of seven witches being executed. The man on the right is the witchfinder being paid by a grateful town council for ridding the area of its witches. (Left) an illustration of the type of magical circle believed by many sorcerers to be essential to their practices.

From many confessions it seemed clear that several covens would often meet together for large ceremonies known as sabbats. It was these which indicated the existence of a widespread and centrally-controlled religion. Witches from a wide area would meet late at night and the festivals begin. The Devil himself was said to appear at sabbats, but the figure reported so often may have been a witch dressed for the part. The ceremonies of the sabbat were marked by wild orgies of drinking, eating and dancing that went on all night.

During the 17th century, some investigators suggested that there was a central authority which controlled all the witches of Europe. Others, however, believed that sabbats were organized locally. Even today, nobody is sure of the truth.

The main problem when trying to find the reality behind these statements and theories is the origin of the statements. Most of the descriptions of esbats and sabbats were given by people on trial for their lives. It is likely that such people would say anything they thought might save them. In addition, many witches were tortured during their trials. It would not be surprising if these poor wretches accused of witchcraft agreed to anything they were asked.

On the other hand, it is almost certain that many country people did make potions. By collecting herbs and wild plants, skilled practitioners could make medicines which would alleviate illnesses and pains. Potions might also be made which were deadly poisons and used to cause death. Any person able to mix such concoctions might be suspected of being a witch. It is also likely that a few people did, in fact, indulge in devil-worship. No doubt they hoped to gain immediate reward from their evil master. It is impossible to know how many confessions were genuine and which were false.

In fact, the actual torture of witches was relatively rare. More often prolonged questioning was used to try to uncover the truth. Persons skilled in such work were known as witchfinders. When magistrates were confronted with someone suspected of being a witch they would send for the witchfinder. Many of these men were honest and dedicated to uncovering the truth. Others seemed obsessed by the fear of witchcraft and were intent on dealing out death to anyone they suspected of being involved.

Perhaps the most infamous witchfinder of all was Matthew Hopkins. Hopkins began his witch hunts in 1645 at Maningtree in Suffolk. He accused a neighbour of being a witch. When she was questioned, the woman named another 32 people as fellow witches. Convinced that witchcraft was rampant in East Anglia, Hopkins set out to destroy it. He travelled round Suffolk, Essex and Norfolk searching out witches.

Grateful town councils paid Hopkins large amounts of money for ridding their boroughs of witchcraft. The prospect of monetary reward seems to have influenced Hopkins' conduct. He became determined to prove a suspect's guilt, even if there was little evidence. The accepted method of detecting a devil's mark was to prick any mole or birthmark with a needle. If it did not bleed, the mark was verified as that of the Devil. Hopkins began using a needle with a retractable point. This made it appear that he was pushing five centimetres (two inches) of steel into a suspect's skin, when no such thing occurred.

In the space of some 14 months, Hopkins sent about 400 people to their deaths on charges of witchcraft. It is not known how many of these people dabbled in magic and potions, but it seems beyond doubt that the vast majority were innocent of any crime. The reign of terror came to an end in the spring of 1646 when John Gaule, a parson, wrote a pamphlet exposing Hopkins' methods. Hopkins was forced to retire and died only a few months later.

After such excesses, the witch trials became less frequent. Finally, in 1736, most of the laws forbidding witchcraft were abolished.

The relaxation of the witchcraft laws were a great step towards tolerance of beliefs. With the threat of execution lifted, many local wise men and women openly prepared herbal remedies. The lack of legal restraint was also seized upon by young noblemen with a taste for defying convention. The most famous of these was Sir

---

The Witch in a Hole

One of the most famous witches in Britain is not actually a human, but a stone. At Wookey in Somerset is a large cave, known as Wookey Hole. Clustered near the entrance are a group of stone pillars which are said to be a witch and her demons turned to stone by a monk. One of the stones does look very much like an old woman with a hooked nose. When the skeleton of an old woman was found in the cave, this seemed to support the old story of the witch of Wookey.

The Brave Minister

Towards the end of the last century the vicar of a small village in Lancashire was riding home late at night. Suddenly the horse stumbled and threw the vicar to the ground, bruising him badly. As the minister struggled to his feet, he heard demonic laughter sounding from close at hand. He knew that the Devil had caused his mount to fall.

"I hear you Satan," called out the brave vicar, "You can laugh when I fall if you like, but when I fall I can get up. When you fell you never rose again."

At these words, which reminded the Devil of his fall from Heaven, a loud groan sounded. The minister was never troubled by the Devil again.

Francis Dashwood who set up a very strange club in the mid-18th century. The group met at Dashwood's house, Medmenham Abbey, and so were known as the Medmenham Monks. The group later gained the more emotive name of the Hellfire Club. Openly defying the practices of established Christianity, Dashwood and his friends indulged in wild parties and semi-serious worship of pagan deities such as Venus. This was, however, very different from traditional witchcraft.

(Right) a group of witches in a ceremony to call up spirits. (Facing page) an ancient manuscript illustration shows the Anglo-Saxon concept of a magician. He is shown grasping a book of spells and presiding over a scene of supernatural bloodshed. In Anglo-Saxon times, magicians were thought to be the masters of demons, not their slaves.

The Murdered Witch

Near Tring, in Hertfordshire, is a spot which most locals avoid after dark. Many years ago a man named Colley became convinced that a neighbour was a witch and had put a curse on him. Colley murdered the supposed witch on the dreaded spot. He was soon arrested and convicted of the killing. As was the custom in those days, he was hanged in chains at the site of his crime. Ever since these tragic events, a large, evil black dog has haunted the site.

(Above) it was once believed that witches could change themselves into animals, as shown in this woodcut of 1489.

Modern Witches

In recent years, witchcraft has undergone a revival. There are now many people who openly acknowledge that they are witches. No doubt many more exist, but do not publicize their activities. The ceremonies of these modern witches are, on the whole, fairly harmless and are far removed from the devil-worship said to have been practised by earlier witches.

The practitioners of modern witchcraft claim that their ceremonies and beliefs are very old indeed. It is said that witchcraft is the ancient pagan religion of pre-Christian Europe. It has even been claimed that the religion dates back to the Stone Age. Some think that witchcraft has remained unchanged since its origins in remote prehistory. Others maintain that the ceremonies have changed greatly over the years, though the basic ideas remained constant.

The modern witches claim that the secrets of their religion are contained in a volume known as the *Book of Shadows*. Copies of this book are supposed to be held only by high priests or priestesses. When a new priest is initiated, he must copy the book out by hand for his own use. In the book are contained instructions for ceremonies, the words of various incantations and the names of the gods.

It is said that the *Book of Shadows* is concerned with magic and ceremony celebrating nature. The changing seasons and the fertility of soil and animals are all emphasized. It is thought that some 100,000 people in the English-speaking world now practise witchcraft. Most of these people sincerely believe that they are part of an ancient religion which is basically good. Other people are not so sure.

For centuries witchcraft was illegal and secret. No books about witchcraft by witches are known to have been written before this century. If any witch had written and published such a book, she would have been instantly arrested and, perhaps, executed. There is no way of proving that the modern ceremonies are older than a hundred years at most.

The man who did much to publicize modern witchcraft and increased the number of covens enormously was Gerald Gardner. He spent much of his early life in Sri Lanka as a colonial official. In 1936 Gardner returned to England and became involved with witchcraft. He claims that in 1939 he met a witch named Dorothy and that he joined her coven.

After several years of active witchcraft, Gardner claims he became a priest and copied out the *Book of Shadows*. In later years, Gardner set up several new covens and published books. In

This modern white witch is casting a spell upon a non-witch who is not present. Together with many other modern witches, she believes that ceremony and ritual can enhance the power of her spells. The candles, arranged in a circle within which she kneels, are believed to release a magical power as they burn gradually lower.

The island of Haiti lies in the West Indies and is a stronghold of voodoo. Thousands of people on the island take part in ceremonies at which spirits are believed to "mount" or possess humans. Dancing, such as that shown here, is an important feature of voodoo rituals and often continues throughout the night until dawn.

these he set out to prove that witchcraft was an ancient religion. Many groups of modern witches claim to be offshoots inspired by Gardner's ideas and practise the ceremonies which he recorded.

However, all these covens depend upon the unsubstantiated claims of Gardner. Many people doubt if he joined a coven led by a woman called Dorothy at all. Even if he did, it is claimed, there is no proof that the coven had any links with ancient witchcraft. Against Gardner it may be said that many of his other writings on folklore and history were rather unsound. He seems to have copied other people's work and to have invented facts. Given this unreliable record, many prefer not to believe Gardner's claims.

However, many modern covens do not claim to have been influenced by Gardner at all. They merely say that they are continuing to practise ceremonies passed on to them by parents and grandparents. Given these claims and counter-claims, it is difficult to be certain about the nature or history of modern witchcraft. However, it is certain that witchcraft is practised.

HORRORS OF THE IMAGINATION

The Storytellers

Stories of terror and suspense have been popular for centuries. People seem to enjoy being frightened by tales of ghosts, monsters and demons. In earlier centuries, when most people could not read, there were no books or magazines to provide these stories. Instead, people would recite such tales from memory.

Many villages would contain one person particularly good at storytelling. He would be in great demand whenever a festival or party was held. And if a person was particularly adept at thrilling people by storytelling and could remember a large number of different tales, he could earn his living in this way. Such men would travel around the country, visiting the castles and courts of noblemen. These rich men were always eager to hear new stories or songs, for live entertainment was much sought after in days before television and books. A good storyteller could be certain of a warm welcome wherever he went.

One of the earliest of these verbal tales to be written down was *Beowulf*. This long story was composed in about AD 700 in England. The story concerns the struggle of an heroic young warrior with a hideous man-eating monster who is causing mayhem by stealing men from a feasting hall. Later the warrior, Beowulf, kills the monster's mother. At the end of the story, Beowulf is killed while trying to slay a huge dragon. The exciting tale must have thrilled those who heard it.

Many other tales of heroic battles with horrific monsters were told at this time and in the following centuries. One of the great advantages of these oral tales was that the storyteller could change them as often as he liked. If an audience did not seem to be enjoying a tale, the storyteller could suddenly introduce a hideous

old witch or a frightening ghost. This livened up the tale and gained the attention of the audience. Another trick often tried by storytellers was to begin a story by saying that it had happened just a short distance away. The location of the tale would alter whenever the teller moved to a different castle.

Whether they invented their own stories, or introduced variations to old tales, the storytellers of old needed to possess quite remarkable memories. They were expected to know hundreds of tales by heart on a variety of subjects. Many of these stories were composed in verse, as if they were enormously long poems, and the storyteller needed to be word perfect.

The storytellers who were able to recite a large number of tales, and who could deliver the stories in an exciting way, became famous men. They were the film stars of their day. One man, named Aneirin, lived in the late 6th century. Not only did he recite tales, but he was also a brave warrior who followed his king into battle and then composed poems about the fighting for that night's feasting.

The skill of storytelling remained important for many centuries, However, the growth of the theatre and the ability to read gradually caused the decline of the storytellers. People became more interested in watching plays or reading books. However, the storytellers left a rich and varied heritage behind them.

Many stories were invented by the storytellers of the Middle Ages, but only a few were ever written down. Of those which have survived, many feature monsters of frightening power and violence. Ghosts, witches and devils are found in other stories. Horror and mystery played a large part in the tales which were recited in the feasting halls of the past.

A master storyteller skillfully relates a tale of monsters and heroes, appearing almost to conjure the horrors into reality with his words.

The Masters of Horror

Since the last century, when ordinary people learnt how to read and write, many horror stories have been written. Some of these stories became immensely popular and have been recognized as great works of literature. Some writers have specialized in horror stories, becoming masters of the art of frightening their readers.

One of the earliest, and in many ways the greatest, of these horror writers was Edgar Allen Poe. Born on 19 January 1809, Poe led a life haunted by tragedy and disaster. Perhaps his own unhappiness gave Poe the inspiration for his many tales of horror.

Poe was orphaned at a young age, but was looked after by John Allan, a Virginian merchant. Educated in London and Virginia, Poe was sent to the University of Virginia. However, Poe began gambling and lost so much money that he had to leave college. In 1830 Poe enlisted at West Point Military Academy, but his wild and lawless behaviour caused his expulsion the following year.

Taking to heavy drinking, Poe slipped into poverty. Though his writings were well known, they brought him little money. What cash Poe did receive, he soon lost through drinking and gambling. In 1836, Poe married his 13-year-old cousin, Virginia Clemm. The pair lived together in abject poverty for 11 years. When Virginia died after a long illness, the loss seems to have broken Poe. He drank even more heavily than usual and died in 1849.

In his short life, Poe managed to gain fame both as a writer and a critic. He produced some magnificent poems and novels. However, it is the short stories which have made Poe so famous. In these, his startling style of writing and weird imagination are given free rein.

In *The Tell-Tale Heart* Poe writes as if he were a demented murderer describing his arrest. The murderer has killed a man and hidden his body beneath the floorboards of his room. When the police arrive to question him, the killer begins to panic. He fancies that the heart of the dead man is beating beneath the floorboards, giving away the crime. The mounting tension in the mind of

(*Above*) *the climax of a story about horrific killings from* Tales of the Rue Morgue *by Edgar Allan Poe. (Right) Edgar Allan Poe, one of the master horror writers of all time. Poe first wrote poetry, but later moved on to write the horror short stories for which he is justly famous.*

the narrator is magnificently described in the short story. It is a masterpiece of psychological writing.

Equally enigmatic and haunting is the tale *William Wilson* in which a man tells the story of

The Horrors of Science

The 20th century has seen an entirely new form of horror literature develop and become popular. This is science fiction. Many tales centre around monstrous alien beasts or on terrifying views of the future. Some writers imagine the future to be dominated by robots and machines, others see the Earth locked in deadly combat with aliens. The boundless realms of science fiction make it a marvellous type of horror.

In the opening scene of The Strange Case of Dr Jekyll and Mr Hyde, *Hyde runs along a street, savagely kicking a young girl to the ground in front of the eyes of horrified onlookers. The tale has become highly successful and popular, and has been used as a basis for a number of films and television programmes.*

a strange man who follows him everywhere, speaking in a weird husky whisper. The surprise ending of this tale is magnificent. In the opening paragraph of another tale, Poe calls it "the most wild yet most homely narrative". It is this mixture of the familiar and the horrific which make Poe's stories all the more terrifying.

Born the year after Poe died, Robert Louis Stevenson became one of the most popular writers of his time. But fame did not come quickly to Stevenson. Until the age of 29, he was pursuing a fairly quiet career as a lawyer. Though several of his works were published, writing remained a second career. But in 1879, Stevenson quarrelled with his father and left his job. Travelling to California, Stevenson became seriously ill. After recovering, he married and returned to Scotland.

The famous scene in The Strange Case of Dr Jekyll and Mr Hyde, *in which the wicked Mr Hyde transforms into the respectable Dr Jekyll.*

In 1882, Stevenson achieved his first great success when he wrote *Treasure Island*. A charming book of children's verse followed. But it was in 1886 that Stevenson entered the world of horror with possibly one of the finest tales of terror ever written.

The Strange Case of Dr Jekyll and Mr Hyde, established Stevenson as a writer of adult fiction. The story came to Stevenson in a nightmare. As soon as he awoke, Stevenson began writing. The whole novel was finished within a week.

The tale of Jekyll and Hyde opens as the friends of Dr Jekyll, one of whom is Dr Lanyon, are becoming increasingly concerned. The respectable Dr Jekyll is strangely linked to an ugly, wicked man named Edward Hyde. It seems clear that Hyde has some sort of power over Jekyll, for the respectable doctor happily pays bills for his disreputable friend. Dr Jekyll has even left all his property to Hyde in his will.

As the story unfolds, Hyde is revealed as a callous man entirely without morals. He is a thoroughly dislikeable person. Dr Jekyll on the other hand is honest and virtuous. The friends of the doctor wonder what possible connection there can be between the two. The truth is revealed one morning to Dr Lanyon, when he is summoned by Mr Hyde.

Lanyon is asked to fetch a glass of medicine, which he does. When Hyde drinks the liquid, he becomes distorted with pain. His whole face changes until he is transformed into Dr Jekyll. The truth is that Jekyll has discovered a drug

which will separate the evil side of his character from the good. In this way, he hoped, he could indulge his wicked fantasies without feeling guilty. However, the idea went wrong when Hyde began to take over completely.

After writing *Jekyll and Hyde*, Stevenson produced many other books and stories. In 1887, Stevenson left Scotland for the Pacific Ocean. After several months cruising, he settled on Samoa. He died on the island in 1894 and his body was buried on the summit of Mount Vaea, overlooking the island he had grown to love.

Another famous horror story to be dreamt into existence is the tale *Frankenstein, or The*

Modern Prometheus. It came to its author Mary Shelley as she lay dozing in a house in Switzerland. Though the book *Frankenstein* was a staggering success and is still popular more than 150 years later, Mary Shelley was not a successful writer. The horror tale was her first work and only work of any repute. The secret of this single achievement may lie in its origins.

Born Mary Godwin, the authoress grew up in England with a father who took no interest in her at all. At the age of 18, Mary Godwin ran off with the 22-year-old poet, Percy Shelley. The couple moved to Switzerland to escape the inevitable scandal, for Shelley was already married. On a July evening 1816, the young couple were staying with Lord Byron and John Polidori. They had been reading ghost stories, and Byron suggested that each of the party try to invent an horrific story.

It was after this that Mary Godwin dozed off and thought of *Frankenstein*. At first she en-

The house where Mary Shelley dreamt of Frankenstein.

visaged only a short story in which a scientist puts together a man from odd pieces taken from dead bodies. As his experiment nears completion, the doctor suddenly regrets his decision and goes to bed. He wakes in the night to find his creation standing beside him. Shelley, however, urged her to expand the story into a full length book.

The resulting novel was a masterpiece. The fascination of the story lies in its subtleness and ambiguity. The artificial man which is created by Baron Frankenstein is not simply a monster. It has a human mind and feelings. The grotesque creature wants nothing more than to be accepted by human society. At first the monster pleads for friendship from Baron Frankenstein and then from other people. But when his suggestions are turned down, the unfortunate fellow becomes embittered and turns against humanity. It is at this point in the story that the monster becomes destructive and murderous.

Throughout the tale, there is a feeling of sympathy for the pathetic creation. He has been called into existence and then abandoned. His dilemma is terrible, yet his reaction is almost as horrible.

Similarly gaining the sympathy of the reader

is Quasimodo, the central character in the novel *The Hunchback of Notre Dame*. Written by the great French writer Victor Hugo, the story appeared in 1831 and is set some four centuries earlier in Paris. Quasimodo is seen in the street by a chaplain of Notre Dame Cathedral. At the time Quasimodo is only a toddler and the chaplain adopts him. Hideously deformed, the hunchback lives within the cathedral and rarely ventures outside. When he does leave the building Quasimodo meets a beautiful girl. From this meeting the story builds up to a dramatic climax.

Of the 20th century writers of horror, two are outstanding. The Frenchman, Gaston Leroux, produced his masterpiece in 1911. The story,

The hunchback of Notre Dame first appeared in the book of that name as an ugly child in the street.

The Phantom of the Opera, was based on the tales of a masked ghost flitting around the magnificent Paris Opera House. However, the identity of the ghost and the tragic story are entirely the creation of Gaston Leroux. So popular did the story become that it has been made into several films and, in 1987, became the basis of a hugely successful stage musical.

The other master of horror of the 20th century was M. R. James. While calling his tales ghost stories, most of James' work was based on other aspects of the supernatural and the occult. Among his more famous works are *Oh, Whistle and I'll Come to You my Lad*, an horrific tale of a haunted whistle, and *Casting the Runes*, which opens with a seemingly innocent letter addressed to a Mr Karswell. The tales of M. R. James have a disturbing quality which makes them masterpieces of horror fiction.

Popular Horror

Though writers such as M. R. James and Edgar Allan Poe are accepted as the masters of horror, they are not as widely known as they might be. Far more popular are the horror stories which are easier to read and to understand.

The earliest truly popular horror tale was *Varney the Vampire, or the Feast of Blood*. The reason for its success was that it was published in cheap, weekly parts which nearly everybody could afford. Appearing in 1847, *Varney the Vampire* was published at the time when reading was becoming a common skill. Before that date relatively few people could read and write more than a few words.

By accompanying the text with lurid and exciting illustrations, *Varney the Vampire* was presented in a way which appealed to ordinary people. Running to an impressive total of 220 chapters, the writing was the work of Thomas Prest, who produced several other serials of great length. The tale reached a stunning climax on the volcanic slopes of Mount Vesuvius and became an instant classic of its type.

Serialized horror stories declined in popularity after *Varney the Vampire* finished its long run. However, horror serials blossomed again in the years following the First World War. In 1922 a magazine with the ominous title *Weird Tales* began publication in the United States. The cover of the magazine always featured a dramatic and horrific scene taken from one of the stories in that month's issue.

Concentrating largely on tales of the occult and witchcraft, *Weird Tales* seemed to have found a subject for which there was an insatiable demand. Perhaps the readership felt that they could be scared by the imaginary tales without needing to take them seriously.

Among the most popular writers in *Weird Tales* were Robert E. Howard, Seabury Quinn and H. P. Lovecraft. Quinn wrote nearly 100 stories for the magazine and was possibly the most popular writer to feature in the publication. Lovecraft was nearly as prolific in his writing, and seems to have been the most influential. He created a complete, yet imaginary, mythology of occult gods. Though Lovecraft knew his characters to be figments of his imagination, others believed that they existed. A few witchcraft covens even invoke these imaginary gods at their ceremonies.

In 1935 a new era of popular horror began. In that year the very first comicbook was published. From the start, the comicbook's mixture of adventure stories contained an element of terror. At first this was found in science fiction tales involving monsters on other planets. But soon traditional horror stories were included, with tales of ghosts and vampires.

In 1937 classic tales began to be translated to the comicbook medium when *The Hunchback of Notre Dame* appeared in *Wags*. Other stories followed, but the Second World War brought an end to the run. After the war, the publication of such works began again. It has continued unabated to the present day.

HORRORS ON THE SCREEN

The Silent Nightmare

A Fool There Was appeared in 1917, starred Theda Bara and became an immense success. It was one of the first films to feature a story involving horror, as Theda Bara played a beautiful woman who preyed on men.

The film industry noted the success of *A Fool There Was* and soon the screens of the world were filled with similar films. A second vampire film to achieve great success was *Nosferatu*, made in 1922 by F. W. Murnau in Germany. The film creates an atmosphere of growing evil as the plot unfolds. Basically, the film follows the plot of the novel *Dracula*. Count Orlock, the vampire character, however, becomes a weird and horrific creature in the film. In this way he is very different from Count Dracula himself. The change of name for the vampire was an attempt to avoid paying royalties to Bram Stoker. The attempt failed and the German producer was forced to pay for the storyline. Interestingly, *Nosferatu* was remade in 1979, again in Germany.

Nosferatu, from the classic 1922 movie.

The silent screen also featured other themes and characters which were to become classics of later films and television features. In 1913 a motion picture filmed on location in Czechoslovakia brought the Devil to the big screen. *The Student of Prague* told the story of a young man who sells his soul to the Devil in return for worldly success.

In 1925 one of the great classic tales of horror appeared in cinemas for the first time. *The Phantom of the Opera* starring Lon Chaney remains one of the finest horror films ever made. Unlike some more recent recountings of the tale, this version stayed close to the original story. The marvellous make-up of Lon Chaney makes the phantom a terrifying figure.

With such films as these, the early cinema exploited the possibilities of horror to the full. Characters and ideas were developed in the silent films which remain popular on today's screens. In some cases, the silent films have never been bettered.

Two actors dominated horror films during the 1930s: (below) Bela Lugosi as Dracula and (facing page) Boris Karloff as Frankenstein's monster.

The First Scream

Magnificent as many of them were, the silent movies lacked one ingredient which can greatly enhance the atmosphere of horror. The missing factor was sound. As soon as a soundtrack was technically possible, horror movies featured the scream of terror.

The first film to use screaming in a truly effective way was *King Kong*, released in 1933 by RKO. The picture tells what happens to a huge ape, found on a remote Pacific island, when it is brought back to New York for exhibition. Here it escapes from its chains and goes on a rampage. The monstrous beast is finally killed after scaling the Empire State Building.

However, the real interest of the film lies in the relationship between King Kong and the beautiful Fay Wray. The monster seems to feel affection for the girl, though his ferocity and power fills her with horror. It is when he grabs the girl that the screaming begins. The ear-piercing yells of Miss Wray echo at length. The tireless duration of her terrified screams and their intensity create much of the atmosphere of the movie. The human scream has been used many times since. Nowadays films are more sophisticated in their treatment of the sound, but few have been as effective.

Two years earlier, a classic movie had been produced by Universal. Screaming played its role in this film too, although not as dominantly as in *King Kong*. The movie was the first talking version of Dracula, which starred Bela Lugosi. Lugosi was the perfect actor to play Count Dracula. He was an East European, had fine aristocratic features and had an almost hypnotic stare. He entered films after serving in the Hungarian cavalry and travelled to America in the 1920s.

He fitted the role of Count Dracula so well that his performance has become the standard by which others are measured. Resplendent in top hat and flowing cape, Lugosi fits in well with the fashionable society of London. But that same cape takes on a sinister air when Dracula reveals himself as the blood-sucking fiend he really is. So well did Lugosi play Dracula, that it was difficult for him to leave the role. A short time

CARL LAEMMLE
presents
FRANKENSTEIN
THE MAN WHO MADE A MONSTER

COLIN CLIVE
MAE CLARKE
JOHN BOLES
BORIS KARLOFF

A UNIVERSAL PICTURE

before his death in 1956, Lugosi was still playing Dracula on stage.

In the same year that Lugosi played Dracula, another great 19th century novel launched a young actor on a distinguished career. The film was *Frankenstein* and the star, Boris Karloff. Though the central character of the film is really Baron Frankenstein who creates the monster, Karloff managed to capture the limelight. His portrayal of the lumbering man-made human was believable and remains so to this day. As in the original book, the monster is not only frightening, but somehow pathetic. Four years later, Karloff played the role again in *The Bride of Frankenstein*.

In 1932, Karloff created another role which has endured for many years. *The Mummy* is a thrilling film which was such a success that a spate of mummy films quickly followed. The most memorable scene in the film comes when an archaeologist is reading an ancient Egyptian scroll. Unknown to him, the scroll contains the incantation designed to bring the mummy back to life. As his voice reaches the end of the spell, a heavy bandaged hand falls on his shoulder. It is one of the great moments of screen horror.

(Below) The Mummy's Tomb *produced in 1943 was the third in Universal's "Mummy" series. (Right) a scene from the 1979 remake of* Nosferatu.

The Terror Continues

After the Second World War the horror movies began to explore new ideas and themes. The old favourites, in the form of Dracula and Frankenstein still featured in various movies. However, it was the new ideas which most excited film-makers and filmviewers alike.

The 1950s were a decade when it seemed that man was at last conquering nature. The idea of nature striking back was one which could make a strong appeal to the imagination. One of the first films to exploit the idea was *The Beast from 20,000 Fathoms* which Warner Brothers made in

1953. The huge monster of the film is a prehistoric giant which lies asleep on the ocean floor. An underwater nuclear explosion awakens the ancient being which then rampages through New York.

A similar theme runs through the film *Them*. In this instance nuclear experiments have created mutations in the form of giant ants. In some ways, the film was one of the best monster movies. The build up of tension is almost unbearable. The film opens with a dazed child stumbling through the desert of the American south west. The child is clearly in a state of shock, and only refers to the horror she has seen

as "them". Police investigators follow a trail of destruction until they come face to face with the giant ants themselves. The mutants are finally disposed of in Los Angeles drains.

A large number of horror films concerning the struggle between man and nature followed these two successes. One of the finest and most successful was *The Birds* released in 1963. This strange film was adapted from a short story by Daphne du Maurier, which told of a family in Cornwall being attacked by murderous flocks of birds. Neither in the story nor the film is any real reason given for the attack, nor is it known whether the event is isolated or whether it is

global in effect. The film concentrates on the mounting horror felt by the family suffering the attacks, which build up to a truly spine-chilling finale.

Another theme often explored in post-war horror movies is that of the future. In 1971 the oddly-titled film *THX 1138* envisaged a world in which humans are programmed to behave almost like robots. The hero of the film is human number THX 1138, who attempts to escape from the system. *Westworld* featured actual robots in its story. The plot is set in a future funpark where robots help the paying public to live out their fantasies. The horror begins when the robots begin to go wrong. One particularly nasty robot, played by Yul Brynner, is a cowboy gunslinger who starts to kill the public.

Also set in the future were the space movies

(Above) a five-metre long ant about to attack in Them! *(Facing page) two scenes from Alfred Hitchcock's classic 1960 movie* Psycho.

which featured various monsters and aliens. In *Alien*, released in 1979, a spaceship stops by a derelict spaceship and unwittingly picks up a ferocious alien creature. As the story slowly unfolds the monster grows in size and kills the crew one by one. Though the film is well made and there are plenty of shocks, the plot is a fairly familiar theme on the lines of a murderous beast on the loose.

Less visually horrific, but far more disturbing was the 1960 film, *Village of the Damned*. Taking its story from the novel by John Wyndham, the film uses no special effects. Instead the aliens

arrive in the form of strange children born in an English village. Only as the youngsters grow up do they reveal their frightening psychic powers. The strangers seem intent upon survival. Anyone who threatens them is swiftly destroyed. When the children's schoolmaster realizes what is happening he destroys them, and himself, with a bomb.

Less disquieting are the monsters which regularly occur in children's films and shows. Of these possibly the most famous are the Daleks. Featuring in the BBC series *Dr Who*, these aliens have featured on the large screen in such films as *Daleks – Invasion Earth 2150*. The Daleks are the robotic casings in which live hideous aliens. Armed with death rays and terrifying metallic voices, the Daleks have thrillingly frightened children for 25 years.

Insanity has been another subject used by the makers of horror films. A picture which showed the way to others was *Arsenic and Old Lace*, made in 1944. The story revolves around two charming old ladies, who happen to be mass-murderers as well. The young man who believes that he is their nephew discovers the old ladies' grisly secret. His mind becomes tortured by the thought that he too might prove to be insane. This engaging and amusing film treats the subject with humour. The same cannot be said of a film *Psycho* made in 1960 by Alfred Hitchcock.

The film's theme is one which can be found in folktales and stories dating back several centuries: a hotel-keeper who is murdering his guests. The film opens as a young woman guest arrives and checks in. She is then savagely murdered in the shower. This murder scene has become a classic of cinema history. Its shocking power and savagery remains constant. The scene

Some horrors return again and again to the cinema screen. (Above left). A Company of Wolves *featured werewolves,* The Thing *(above) and* Alien *(left) concerned a space monster which attacked humans.*

is all the more remarkable for the lack of gory detail shown. The horrific effect is created by suggestion and implication.

A growing trend in horror films has been the introduction of humour. In some cases the amusement is contained in otherwise serious stories. When offered wine in one of his many screen appearances, Dracula remarks "I don't drink" and then adds "wine" with a significant glance. In a moment from a Frankenstein movie, the monster is chided with the words "You have a civil tongue in your head, I know, I sewed it there." However, some films are total comedies, while still dealing with traditional horror themes.

In recent years horror movies have become increasingly gory and violent. (Above) a gruesome walking corpse from Dawn of the Dead. *(Facing page)* Carrie *made in 1976.*

In 1948 the American comedy team Abbot and Costello featured in *Abbot and Costello meet Frankenstein*. The comedy in this film swamped the horrific element, provided by Bela Lugosi, and the film today appears to be rather childish and unfunny. The much later *Young Franken-stein*, made in 1974, is more amusing. Perhaps this is because the film maintains an air of horror alongside its humour.

Very different, and to some minds, even funnier was the strange film *Time Bandits*. The film opens as a mounted knight in armour crashes out the bedroom wardrobe of a young boy. The out-of-place knight then gallops off

into a forest which does not exist and vanishes. In the course of the film, the boy is taken on a frantic trip through time meeting such charac-ters as Robin Hood and Napoleon, and is threatened by a savage minotaur. The film reaches a startling climax in a battle against the Devil in which the boy plays a part.

It seems that horror can be both frightening and amusing.

Acknowledgements

Aldus Archive/BPCC 96, 100 bottom (Bodleian Library); BBC Hulton Picture Library 90 right, 94, 95 bottom, 112; 'Britain on View' (BTA/ETB) 48–9; The British Library 101; Camera Press 102, 103; Jean-Loup Charmet 97 bottom (Bibliothèque Nationale); courtesy of The Essex Institute, Salem, MA 93 bottom, 95 top; Mary Evans Picture Library 90 left, 91, 106; Fortean Picture Library/Janet & Colin Bord 54–5; John Freeman & Co/Fotomas Index 98 bottom; Hamlyn Group Picture Library 15, 19, 34–5, 39, 42 inset, 42–3, 46–7, 47 inset, 73, 83 inset, 97 top; Hammer Films 82–3; Pat Hodgson Library 93 top; The Kobal Collection 67, 114, 115 inset, 116 left, 116–7, 118, 119 top, 119 bottom, 120 top, 120–1, 121 top, 122, 123; The Mansell Collection 27, 98 top, 107; John Murray (Publishers) Ltd 110; National Trust: Jeremy Whitaker 17; Popperfoto 92; Ann Rownan Picture Library 100 top; Stills Library/National Film Archive 113, 115; Judy Todd 88, endpapers; University of London, Harvey Price Library 58 top, 58–9, 59 top; ZEFA 84–85; the illustration of Glamis Castle (36–37) is reproduced by courtesy of the Rt Hon Earl of Strathmore and Kinghorne.

Cover illustration
Peter Dennis

INDEX